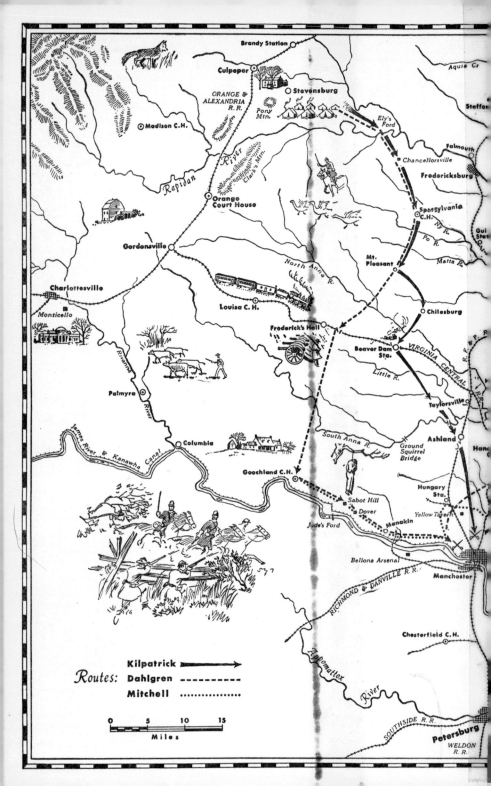

Brandy Station

Culpeper

ORANGE & ALEXANDRIA R.R.

Stevensburg

Pony Mtn.

Madison C.H.

Ely's Ford

Aquia Cr.

Stafford

Chancellorsville

Falmouth

Fredericksburg

Clark's Mtn.

Rapidan River

Orange Court House

Spotsylvania C.H.

Gui Sta.

Po R.

Ny R.

Gordonsville

North Anne R.

Mt. Pleasant

Matta R.

Charlottesville

Louisa C.H.

Frederick's Hall

Chilesburg

VIRGINIA CENTRAL

Monticello

Beaver Dam Sta.

Little R.

Rivanna River

Palmyra

Taylorsville

Ashland

South Anna R.

Columbia

James River & Kanawha Canal

Goochland C.H.

Ground Squirrel Bridge

Han

Hungary Sta.

Sabot Hill

Dover

Jude's Ford

Manakin

Yellow Tavern

Bellona Arsenal

Manchester

RICHMOND & DANVILLE R.R.

Chesterfield C.H.

Appomattox River

Routes:

Kilpatrick ——→

Dahlgren - - - -

Mitchell ·········

0   5   10   15

Miles

SOUTHSIDE R.R.

Petersburg

WELDON R.R.

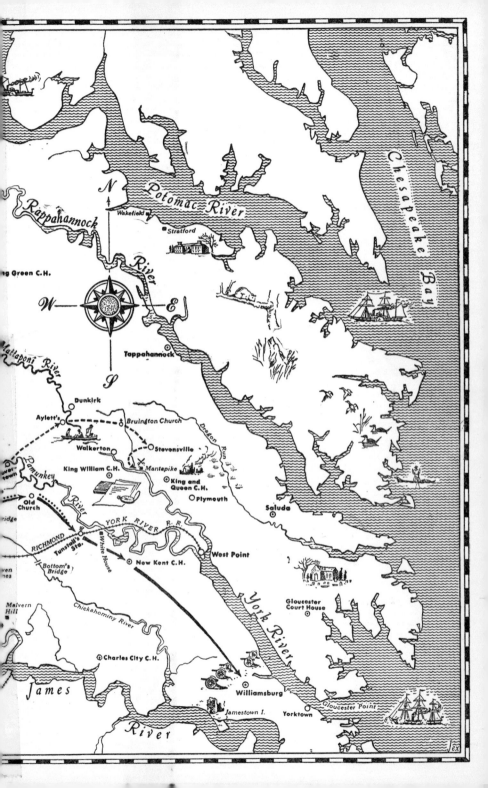

Eight Hours Before Richmond

Eight Hours

By VIRGIL CARRINGTON JONES

Before Richmond

Introduction by Colonel Robert Selph Henry

Illustrated with Photographs

HENRY HOLT AND COMPANY • NEW YORK

To E. Huber (Duke) Ulrich, the boss who has put up with me longer than any other of my experience . . . except my wife

Foreword

IN EARLIER BOOKS Virgil Carrington Jones has given vivid and absorbing accounts of the exploits of Southern guerrilla leaders in the eastern theater of the War Between the States—Mosby, White, Hanson, Gilmor, and their commands. In the present volume he turns to an exploit of Union arms which came to a climax in the "eight hours before Richmond" of the title.

During these hours, from 10:00 A.M. of Tuesday, March 1, 1864, until dark of the same day, Richmond was threatened by a two-pronged attack of mounted forces led by twenty-eight-year-old Brigadier General Judson Kilpatrick, striking from the north, and by twenty-one-year-old Colonel Ulric Dahlgren, coming in from the west. Both forces penetrated into the very suburbs of the almost undefended capital of the Confederacy, but neither managed to achieve any part of the planned objective of releasing the thousands of Union soldiers held prisoner on Belle Isle and in Libby Prison.

From the genesis of the idea in Kilpatrick's fertile brain, there had been military misgivings. General Pleasonton, his immediate superior, had declared the project to be "not feasible." General Meade, commanding the Army of the Potomac, regarded the undertaking as "desperate" but thought, nevertheless, that Richmond might be carried by a rapid and secret *coup de main* and the prisoners be released before reinforcements could be brought from either Lee's Army or Petersburg. At any rate, as he wrote his wife, the "anxiety and distress of the public and the authorities at Washington" over reports as to the condition of the prisoners was "so great that it seems to demand running great risks for the chances of success." If succesful, moreover, it would be "the greatest feat of the war."

Young Dahlgren, starting on the expedition which Kilpatrick had conceived and persuaded President Lincoln and Secretary Stanton to approve, realized the risks but felt that it would succeed and if so, it would be "the grandest thing on record." The state of mind of the author of the plan himself may be gathered from a newspaper account of a message he was said to have sent to Pleasonton after the column of some 4000 men was safely across the Rapidan: "Twenty miles nearer Richmond, and all right. Will double my bet of $5,000 that I enter Richmond."

And perhaps he would have done it, Richmond being all but undefended, had it not been for a series of errors in judgment, compounded by a storm of rain, sleet, snow, and rising streams, and clinched by failure of resolution when, at the critical time, he failed to hear sounds of Dahlgren attacking from the south as planned. Then and thereafter, the raid—in Mr. Jones' phrase—"completely went to pieces."

Why this operation, which had "seemed so simple on paper, so foolproof" when Kilpatrick had outlined it in person to the President and the Secretary of War, came to such complete and utter failure is developed in detail in Mr. Jones' study of the course of events and the character of its leader.

Failing in his purpose, Kilpatrick turned away from Richmond to seek refuge behind the battalions of Ben Butler in the direction of Williamsburg. Dahlgren, who had tried to enter Richmond from the west because he had been unable to cross the James so as to come in from the south as originally planned, did not rejoin Kilpatrick's main body but sought safety further north, aiming for Gloucester Point. Struggling through the mud and the darkness near King and Queen Courthouse, his column was ambushed by Virginia home guards and Dahlgren himself was killed.

But the story does not end with Dahlgren's death or even with the burning of the village near which he was killed in retaliation, for there were found upon Dahlgren's body (or if the Northern contention be accepted, there were placed upon his body) three documents—an address to his "Officers and Men," a set of instructions to a separate portion of his command, and a memorandum book containing entries from which portions of the address and the instructions seemed to have been drawn.

The address contained an exhortation to the command not only to release the Union prisoners from Belle Isle but also to "cross the James River into Richmond . . . exhorting the released prisoners to destroy and burn the hateful city; and do not allow the Rebel leader Davis and his traitorous crew to escape." In the detailed instructions, it was said that the city "must be destroyed and Jeff. Davis and Cabinet killed," to which there was added, in the notebook, an admonition that this must be done "on the spot."

The genuineness of the documents has been a matter of controversy for nearly a century. It was stoutly denied by the North, largely on the ground that the address to the command had not been issued and, besides, that it was signed "U. Dahlgren" instead of "Ulric Dahlgren," and as stoutly maintained by those who found and transmitted the documents. Mr. Jones examines both positions and, from the statement of those concerned and the internal evidence of the papers themselves, comes to the conclusion that the disputed documents were not Confederate forgeries but were genuine.

Raids were a notable feature of the war of the '6os—long-distance raids deep into enemy territory, as well as quick stabs behind opposing armies. Richmond itself was the object of more than one of these efforts, but no raid was more dramatic and more nearly successful, and none left behind more of controversy and unresolved questions, than the Kilpatrick-Dahlgren raid which is so thoroughly, capably, and interestingly brought to life in Eight Hours Before Richmond.

ROBERT SELPH HENRY
President, the Southern
Historical Association

Alexandria, Virginia
August 28, 1957

Contents

Eight Hours Before Richmond

1

Fun and Foreboding

THERE WAS EVERY REASON why the Washington's Birthday Ball should be a great occasion for members of General George G. Meade's proud, untarnished old II Corps. For many of them it would be their last chance to dance. The winter of 1864 was in its last stages, and soon, when the roads had dried, the North would expect its blue-clad hordes to march off in a final drive at Lee's thinned and starving army. It must be the end: the war had lasted nearly three years, much too long a period for a nation to devote to civil strife. But nearer at hand, bearing greater urgency and perhaps bringing quicker death to some of them, was a projected raid on Richmond. Most of the details of this undertaking were still in the rumor stage, and yet certain of them had been repeated often enough to have taken on some degree of authority. It was whispered that the movement was designed to free Federal prisoners holed up in the Rebel capital, and that it would be led by Brigadier General Judson Kilpatrick. This last would seem to be borne out by the fact that his barnstorming cavalrymen were scheduled to take part in a giant review the day after the dance.

It was in this atmosphere of expectancy that the II Corps-men went about plans for the ball. Their surroundings were not exactly suited to an interlude of gaiety; in fact they conceded that perhaps no worse setting for such a festive occasion could be found than the camps of the Army of the Potomac around Brandy Station and Culpeper and Stevensburg, deep in Virginia's Piedmont area. Nearly everybody there lived in tents, most of them miles away from the points where the brave little locomotives, with their noisy cylinders, screechy whistles, and bulbous smokestacks, chugged in from the Union capital sixty-odd miles away. Some of the roads that had to be traversed seemed without bottom, and mud was everywhere. But any soldier could take his sweetheart in arms and wade through muck above his ankles; and both officers and privates were determined nothing should stand in the way of the ball. These veterans, hardy fighters who had trekked back triumphantly from Gettysburg the previous summer, wanted to dance, and dance they would, all inconveniences to the contrary.

For weeks work continued on a building to be used as a sort of temple of joy. There the exciting ball would be held, and there the visiting ladies would see what this army life was all about. Under its roof officers with heavy boots and broad mustaches, noisy sabers and jingling spurs, would dance the reel and the polka and the waltz, whispering promises it was a long-odds chance death would never permit them to fulfill.

In the early planning, a sawmill near Culpeper was commandeered, and men with experience as loggers went deep into the woods after lumber-bearing trees from which to build their dance hall. Back and forth they sweated and cursed, storming at balky army horses and mules, laboring over rough terrain, getting stuck in the mud, thrashing through bushes and briers, sometimes becoming entangled in Virginia's vibrant growth of wild grapevine, but all the while snaking out the best trees they could find. These were hauled to the protesting saw, which, sharpened all too infrequently, ripped them into planks of every length and width. As the lumber pile mounted, the carpenter element swung into action and worked on a dawn-to-dark schedule. Gradually, above the muck and mire, arose a structure one hundred feet long and fifty feet wide, temporary to the last degree. Beneath its roof would be housed more fun and frolic per cubic foot than in any other building throughout northern Virginia.[1]

February 22 fell on Monday; the influx of girls began the preceding Friday. These early arrivals set up the social stride for a busy week end. Trysts were broken and new ones made, hearts smashed and others healed, all in a great aura of excitement and laughter, love-making and loneliness, which go to make up an off-hour of a huge army. Here in a giant arena of tents and kettles, flagpoles and headquarters wagons, uniforms and bugle notes, was staged the major event of the winter's social whirl, a great merriment to hide for a moment the self-abasement of a nation. The motif for the celebration was military to the last shiny button on the uniform of the last happy soldier preparing himself for the rough pine-board dance floor. And while the gaiety was in progress, guns waited in silence along the Rapidan River, stared down upon by the signal officers stationed on Pony, Clark's, Garnett's and Stony Mountains. It was strong allegiance to duty that these fellows up on the high bulwarks were showing, for they stood at their posts and tried to concentrate on war dangers while their thoughts kept turning to high-heeled shoes and hoop skirts, sachet powder, ruby lips, and shoulder curls.

Among the first guests to arrive, on an express train especially reserved for the purpose, was Mrs. Curtin, wife of the stormy governor of Pennsylvania, bringing with her a bevy of beauties—including her own daughter—from Washington and beyond. Wrote an officer captivated by her daughter's charms: "Miss Curtin, a graceful, beautiful girl, is easily the belle of the party and attracts universal attention. She is certainly magnificent, dignified, sweet, and graceful in her demeanor." [2]

Also among the early arrivals at Brandy Station was a young man who hobbled painfully down the steps of a coach and made his way along the platform paying little notice to the incoming celebrants. He was Colonel Ulric Dahlgren, son of Rear Admiral John A. Dahlgren, the Scandinavian now famous as a world authority on ordnance, the inventor of a powerful, bottle-shaped gun, and commander of the Union fleet besieging Charleston down in South Carolina. The newcomer, who was nearing his twenty-second birthday, was obviously not there to dance, for he stumbled along on crutches and a wooden leg. As soon as a horse was made available to him, he climbed awkwardly into the saddle, strapped the crutches beneath his good leg, and struck off toward Stevensburg and Kilpatrick's headquarters. Dahlgren may have been arriving early to be as inconspicuous as possible; but his presence, it developed, was living evidence that the plan of a raid on Richmond was pretty generally known in Washington.

Many of the female guests were assigned to tents, two to each, with servants to attend their wishes. Of a morning, while the girls stretched and nerved themselves to come squealing out from under the warm, heavy covers, soldiers appeared on the scene to build fires, bring hot water, clean boots, and attend to the rougher of the camp chores. Then a band marched out in front of the quarters to serenade the ladies during the painfully long period they spent at their toilets.

At mess call, officers formed to escort the ladies to their places. Each guest was sandwiched in between two men, all of them chattering and excited and gleefully happy. At the head of each and every table, presiding in suave and graceful manner, sat a general. Two hours to a meal was average.

Cornelia Hancock, Quaker nurse who in afteryears was to become famous for her letters written from the Army of the Potomac, was one who felt the pressure of this influx of visitors. Trusted to her care were seven Washington women, and she commented for the record that she was glad it had become warmer, "or I fear they would perish." Officers in great numbers passed her house in the woods. "There is only one official more who is needed here," she wrote her mother. "That is someone to escort visitors around. Neither the surgeon or myself can bear the task and it is laughable what a skedaddling there is when visitors appear: but one of us has to take it. If it did not come so often it would not be so bad." [3]

Over at Stevensburg, in the tree-bordered mansion serving as Kilpatrick's headquarters, the welcome mat and the grand manner were much in evidence.[4] Kilpatrick aspired to be a major general, so the most important guests were gathered beneath his roof, including many United States senators—the public officials who must give final approval to the commissions of general officers.

One guest who accepted Kilpatrick's invitation was Hamilton Gay Howard, son of and secretary to Senator Jacob Howard of Michigan. To this nineteen-year-old seeking a college education, the cavalry leader seemed to be "a little man, with loud, swaggering voice, full of fun and profanity, florid face, square prognathous jaw, firm, large mouth, prominent Roman nose, quick, deep-set, piercing, fearless gray eyes, full, square forehead, large round head, large ears, dark, thin and short hair." [5]

Howard had the "good fortune" to be invited to share two mattresses with eight staff officers and newspaper correspondents in the attic of the home. At some time or other this part of the house had been invaded by a cannon ball that left a trail of damage, tearing through the wall and floor. The hole in the wall had been handsomely closed, but the hole in the floor was merely covered over with loose boards and sealed below with ordinary newspapers pasted to the ceiling.

After an opening night of feasting, music, and extemporized Negro minstrels, the attic occupants ascended to their quarters. There they were, lounging in various positions, enjoying a last smoke before sleep, when the musical laughter of women came to their ears from below. This was temptation, and they gave immediate attention. Silently they removed their shoes, doused the light, took away the boards, and began wetting their fingers and noiselessly punching holes in the newspapers.

"Soon we had made quite a rent in the paper ceiling," Howard recorded, "and as it gradually grew larger by frequent application of wet fingers, the laughter below suddenly ceased and our eyes were shortly ravished by seeing a noted beauty of New York City in white, open-necked nightrobe, holding a lighted candle aloft and shedding its rays over her lovely face, bosom, and falling mass of golden hair, approach and, with a mystified and innocent look, gaze up at the rent we envious Cascas had made in the paper ceiling 'mantle' that had shielded her privacy."

This started a fracas. Brooms were brought into play from down below, and a battle royal raged through the gaping hole left by the cannon ball. On and on it went, with much laughter, until the men sued for quarter by lowering half a dozen bottles of wine.

Days of the week end were taken up with a wide assortment of diversion, including sports and riding. Capable riders among the women had sent down their saddles and moved about on horseback, while the others were transported in ambulances. However and wherever they went, in close proximity followed cooks with an abundance of viands and wines. Through the vast fields of canvas villages they were escorted, and some of them were taken on excursions to the front, there to peep across the Rapidan in the direction of Rebel pickets in the distance.

Many distinguished guests were on hand. Vice-President Hannibal Hamlin arrived with his daughter, Sarah, looked upon as a most agreeable young lady. Mrs. Kate Chase

Sprague, considered by some the handsomest woman in Amer-
ica, arrived, and so did her husband, the governor of Rhode
Island. A large party appeared from the British Embassy.
Mrs. Chancellor Walworth, socialite, detrained from New
York. O. A. Brownsen, journalist, was there to represent his
popular publication, *Brownsen's Review*. Families of United
States senators were numerous. Senator Zach Chandler of
Michigan came in by train, and so did Senator Wilkinson of
Minnesota. Even some of the judges of the Supreme Court
laid aside their law books to partake of the fun.

Down from Washington by train were transported special
shipments of food and liquors to be served throughout the fes-
tivities. The capable hands of professionals were everywhere
in evidence. Gautiers, the name looked for in catering, supplied the dishes for General Meade's table.

Not to miss an opportunity in the presence of so many
celebrities, especially those from the halls of Congress, an assembly for oratory was held in a public building in Culpeper.
The most colorful of the speeches was made by Kilpatrick,
the amateur orator-actor, who stirred up great enthusiasm by
hinting that something momentous was about to happen. Officers and privates and even a scattering of women were in
the audience, and the glitter of rich uniforms and fancy at-
tire was prominent. At one point in the program a soldier in
the overcoat of an enlisted man slipped in from the wings and
took a seat at the back of the platform. He was retiring and
unobtrusive and, when later he removed his heavy coat, he
bared the dress uniform of a brigadier general. It was Wesley
Merritt, rising in stature and, before the year was out, to be
heard from in the Shenandoah Valley as an important cavalry
leader. But Merritt was there only to listen: the secret enterprise coming up was Kilpatrick's, the laurels of which were
not to be shared with a fellow brigadier.[6]

On the day of the ball things of note also were happening
south of the Rapidan, over in Confederate circles. While sev-

eral hours of daylight were still left, General Robert E. Lee, commanding the South's Army of Northern Virginia, boarded a train for Richmond to confer with President Jefferson Davis on the military outlook.

Night came on, and the hour finally neared for the band to strike up in the newly erected dance hall. Officers scurried to round up their partners. Ambulances and other vehicles, including heavy equipment and even sidesaddles, were in general use, transporting the ladies through the Virginia mud. By the time the dance was in full swing, 300 females of varying ages were present.[7]

As the women walked with a rustle of sweeping skirts into the giant chamber, the smell of new-cut pine came strongly to their nostrils, and their dainty slippers were pitiful misfits against the rough boards of the floor. But the revelers, male and female, were thankful for what the army had been able to provide, and from them universally came cries of admiration at the sight of the decorations. On all sides a sea of bunting, illuminated with clusters of candles and strings of Chinese lanterns, brought into focus the hugeness of the affair. Regimental and headquarters flags hung overhead in a multitude of colors, each a silent legacy that stimulated thoughts of bloody battles, roaring cannon, smoking guns, and dying men. At one side a raised platform, appropriately lighted, provided a camp scene that blended with the mood of the evening: shelter tents drawn tight, highly polished rifles in ornamental groups, two shiny brass Napoleons, drums and bugles, and around them all the utensils and accouterments of a well-furbished billet.

General Meade was there, having arrived by ambulance from his headquarters five miles away. So was his son, George, braced for an evening in which he would enjoy himself "hugely." [8]

As the evening wore along, louder and louder became the uproar from the dance hall. Socialites were swung about in a grand free-for-all, without note of rank held by the men who chose them as partners. Around Brandy, for this one evening, war worries and military routine got little attention. In the midst of the hilarity a woman, approached by a cavalry general, muttered condolences over the recent death of his soldier son. Smilingly the officer replied, without change of expression: "Yes, madam, very sad. He was the last of his race. Do you waltz?" And away they glided, his huge saber clattering against the legs of other dancers and his spurs reflecting a wicked gleam in the mellow light from the candles and Chinese lanterns.[9]

The occasion caught Hamilton Howard in lyrical mind, a mood he preserved until he could get to his diary. "Gayly sped the feet and sweetly smiled the lips of the brave and beautiful and honored of the republic," he recorded. "Swiftly passed the hours of the festal night, and with the mating song of lark and blue bird and the courtesies of parting, the morning light looked in upon a banquet hall deserted."

General Meade got to bed at 4:00 A.M. Beneath the stars, frosty and pale and cheerless, a crisscross of ambulances and army wagons and horses went out to convey less important figures to their quarters. Attentive men in uniform and tired young ladies in wilted gowns were brought for the moment closer to reality than they had been for hours. But it was sweet parting to them, for in a short time they would be back together for more of the exciting entertainment arranged on the plains of Brandy Station.

At eleven o'clock in the morning, after a modicum of sleep, Meade climbed to his saddle and rode out for a giant review staged by II Corps. At the site chosen for the spectacle he found throngs of people waiting. Then bugles sounded, officers barked, and the band played as column after column swung past in a glittering array. Artillery with shining guns on the carriages and blue-coated and red-striped soldiers on the caissons. Grim, bronzed infantry in dark blue uniforms and slouch hats. Cavalry in lighter blue and yellow trimming.

And skirting the entire line of march the officers in dark blue, red, and gold. But the heart and bulk of the massive exhibition was the private soldier, flashing his military finery for the benefit of his officers' lady friends. And then in the late afternoon Kilpatrick, the ambitious general soon to be making history for the newspapers, came leading his cavalry in a thunderous charge of flashing sabers and flying hoofs, a fitting and nerve-tingling climax to a display of might.

When the parade was over, the party broke up, and soldier and citizen turned away to face the realities of war. Certain signs were in the air, signs that indicated the spring offensive was not far away. Some of these were obvious, some would prove obvious only in retrospect, and several had appeared as recently as the last few hours. Yet, tangible or intangible, they supported the belief that something momentous, as Kilpatrick had indicated in his speech, was in the offing. One of these was a telegram from Rufus Ingalls, Meade's chief quartermaster, directing officers in Washington to send ten gallons of turpentine, in strong two-gallon cans, and one hundred pounds of oakum to Brandy Station the very next day after the ball. But a more obvious portent was the fact that Ulric Dahlgren, a young officer usually seen where there was action, stayed on at Kilpatrick's headquarters after the great celebration had ended.

2

Background for Daring

THE IDEA FOR the rumored dash on Richmond had originated with Kilpatrick, but it was not new. Only a few weeks before, another such expedition had been engineered by bungling Ben Butler, the Union general commanding at Fortress Monroe. This earlier venture had wound up in complete failure, through no fault of the officer in charge, and the mistakes connected with it were a sort of inspiration that helped in laying out details for Kilpatrick's raid.

Basically, both expeditions could be traced to identical influences: idleness in the camps during the cold months, giving officers the opportunity to think up wild schemes, and an outburst of disturbing reports on the treatment accorded Federal prisoners held at the Confederate capital. Most of the winter the armies had been shut up in tents and huts and barracks, staring at each other in boredom day after day and occasionally firing a musket or lobbing over a heavy shell, just to let it be known they still were in business. As the calendar turned to a new year, there was revived talk of effort on the part of President Abraham Lincoln to bring the war to a close. The

Rebels seemed to have had their backs broken at Gettysburg, and since then they had withdrawn into Virginia below the Rapidan to await a break in the weather, only now and then striking out with flank action to worry the Union high command. General Meade, the Federal officer of highest rank, was perhaps as well trained and soldierly an individual as any who had held the office, but somehow he lacked the spark and dash needed to bottle up Lee's army. For weeks he had been confined at Philadelphia with lung inflammation, and this period of inactivity added nothing to his reputation.

During the winter lull General John Hunt Morgan, the exciting Confederate raider, arrived in Richmond, and his presence gave a stir to things. It had been several weeks since his escape from the Federal prison at Columbus, Ohio, where he had been confined since his disastrous raid into the Northwest the preceding summer, and the details of his feat were generally known. They made of him a hero for whom martial music filled the streets; and some of his men, many of them huge Kentuckians, took part in a welcoming parade. The Southerners noted that he had been treated not as a prisoner of war but as a common felon, with head shaved.

Meanwhile a stir of another kind was being created by Morgan's opposite number. Lodged down in Libby, the officer prison on the banks of the James, was Colonel A. D. Streight, one of the Union's most distinguished raiders. With a provision brigade of troops, a good number of them inexperienced riders and some mounted on mules, he had ripped through the deep South, with general destruction his aim, until he was attacked and overwhelmed by Nathan Bedford Forrest. Soon after Streight's imprisonment, Morgan had been captured, and the North immediately announced the Rebel leader and his men would be held as hostages for the good treatment of the Federal officer. But now Morgan was free, and that left the Union holding the bag.

Streight spent much of his time complaining of the treatment accorded him and his fellow prisoners. He claimed that it was "entirely contrary to all civilized usages," and urged the Federal government to do something about it.[1] Six hundred men, he said, were confined in crowded quarters, while rations were of the semistarvation variety—only a quarter-pound of fresh beef, half-pound of bread, and half-gill of rice or beans per day. He reported that solely through purchases made on the outside, at exorbitant prices and with the aid of their guards, were they able to sustain themselves in their close prison confinement, and even then scorbutic diseases were beginning to appear.

It was the last of August, '63, when Streight made his charges, and throughout the early fall there were denials and counterdenials. Colonel James M. Sanderson, who had served in the Union Commissary Department, issued a statement praising the type of rations issued prisoners. He was promptly denounced by a mass meeting of the officer inmates. Then came a note to Secretary of War Edwin M. Stanton in Washington. It was from Bishop J. Johns of the Protestant Episcopal Church in Virginia, written "with no other design than to subserve the cause of humanity," and it stated that the churchman, on his visits to the prison, had inquired of the men individually if they had any cause to complain. The replies, he said, were uniformly negative. Then he had asked if there was anything they wanted. Yes, two things, they answered: outdoor exercise and to go home.

Others had a different report. Lieutenant Colonel William Irvine of the Tenth New York Cavalry wrote that "our men held as prisoners here are suffering and dying from exposure for the want of necessary clothing, and their condition is daily becoming worse and worse." Brigadier General Neal Dow of the United States Volunteers, who thought himself the only general officer the Rebels held, complained mostly of the food: "The entire ration is a piece of hoecake six by four and a half inches and one inch thick, one sweet potato, small size and poor quality, and water."

But that was in the early fall. After the middle of November there was little dispute about conditions in Richmond prisons. From that period on they got worse and worse. An official Confederate report around this time showed 1044 men housed in a building that formerly had held 600. The daily ration was listed as a pound of bread, half-pound of meat, half-pound of potatoes, rice, or beans, vinegar and salt, plus at one meal soup made from the water in which the meat had been boiled. Provisions were weighed and measured to messes of a hundred men each and were delivered to one member of each group assigned to receive and distribute it. This report admitted there might be cases of hardship, but contended these were unavoidable in the management of such a number of men, that they could be traced to accident, to abuse of authority by a subordinate officer, to neglect of the prisoner himself, or to cruelty of his fellow prisoners.

But if the officers in Libby thought they had cause for complaint, they should have been over on Belle Isle with the privates. That waterbound tract of land dividing the James River just opposite the Oregon Hill section of Richmond could hardly be characterized as a human habitat; and even more discouraging to prisoners quartered there was the view of the Confederate capitol, a column-fronted building staring down like a watchdog from an elevation in the center of the city. Also in plain view, a haunting temptation to men longing for freedom, were the Richmond & Petersburg and the Richmond & Danville Railroads, a spur of the latter crossing the river to the island.

Belle Isle at one time had been a well-conducted prison camp, with streets laid off in an orderly manner, tents aligned, sanitary conditions attended to daily, and control over prisoners efficiently maintained. Then Southern victories brought from 6000 to 10,000 men to be crowded onto an island large enough to accommodate scarcely a third that number, and that was when the blight began. To prevent escape, inmates were not allowed to visit the sinks at night, a restriction that forced them to put their deposits of excrement in the streets and in small vacant spaces between the tents. During the day, when police details came along to remove the filth, the area was so crowded they could not properly attend to their work. The situation was made worse by the type of individual quartered there. Many were foreigners fighting for the North in return for bounty, and this meant that they were devoid of nationalism, sentiment, or patriotism. When General Dow was allowed to visit the island to supervise distribution of clothing sent down on a mercy ship from Washington, he was met by such profane abuse from the prisoners that he turned to the Confederate officer in charge and remarked, "You have here the scrapings and rakings of Europe." [2]

Cold weather aggravated hardships to the extreme. Not enough tents were available to shelter the men, and many of them were without a single blanket. Food got scarce. In January eleven days passed without a morsel of meat. Bread made of unsifted meal caused a flagrant epidemic of diarrhea and dysentery. With these ailments were mixed typhoid fever, catarrh, erysipelas, debility, double pneumonia, and scorbutus. Patients who had never attended sick call were brought out on litters, unable to walk and greatly emaciated. Medical officers were unable to keep track of the sick. Dozens of patients from the island died each month in Richmond hospitals within twenty-four hours after they were admitted, most of them speechless and delirious, their names pinned to their clothing whenever the conductor of ambulances could establish their identity. In one month 337 victims of chronic diarrhea were admitted to one hospital, and of these 265 died. [3]

In its defense the South cited that Confederate prisoners confined in the North were undergoing treatment "infinitely worse, more inhuman, uncivilized and barbarous" than any accorded Union captives held in Richmond. Specific cases were cited. Southerners were required to perform hard labor and, if they refused, were tied up by their thumbs. Fifteen Rebel officers were confined in a room fifteen feet square, aired by only a simple slit in the wall, and were forced to perform the operations of nature in a tub removed only once every twenty-four hours.[4] Others were forced to do such filthy labor as cleaning privies while weighted down by ball and chain. And John Morgan had been dressed in convict's clothing, a debasement not yet visited on Streight.

The South further cited that it had always desired a prompt and fair exchange of prisoners. This was agreed to by the North as long as the preponderance of captives rested with the Rebels. When the fortunes of war transferred this balance to the Union, Washington authorities refused further exchange. But, anyway, things would have to stay as they were in Richmond until a new prison pen could be completed down at Andersonville, Georgia. Besides, the Confederacy had no tents, no blankets, no food to supply the prisoners on Belle Isle—or even its soldiers in the field. Southern newspapers, noting the shortage of bread and beef, frankly discussed the possibility of general famine.[5] And a joint select committee of the Confederate Congress, appointed to investigate conditions in the Richmond prisons, blandly observed: "How often the gallant men composing the Confederate army have been without meat!"

It was this situation—the North tightening its strangle hold and the South helpless to avoid the effect—that made a dash on Richmond seem worthwhile. Anything to get those starving men off Belle Isle and the cramped officers out of Libby!

General Butler, in mapping out plans for his attempt on Richmond, had depended largely on information snaked out by spies inside the city. One of these was Elizabeth Van Lew. "Miss Lizzie," or "Crazy Bet" as some folks called her, was stanch to the old flag. She equipped herself and her home for

a long siege of espionage. She sought out people with sympathies akin to her own, and she arranged secret passageways
and secret rooms in the large old mansion she occupied in the
Church Hill section of the city, only a short distance from the
spot where Patrick Henry had made his "Give me liberty or
give me death" speech. Throughout the war she operated,
member of a prominent family, calling herself a Southerner,
and sometimes, to confuse her neighbors, acting a bit de-
mented. Her undercover work was so effective that it earned
her the admiration of highest Union officials, military and
civilian; and her methods were so thorough that never at night
did she lie down to sleep without placing at the side of her
bed all papers of an incriminating nature, so they could be
destroyed at a moment's notice.[6]

It was from Miss Van Lew's concealed chambers that a
messenger one day went out toward Butler's lines. Tucked in
his clothing was a message of vague importance, as well as an
identifying token that gave assurance the carrier could be
trusted. He moved with an urgency impressed upon him by
Betty. This was a crisis only she could perceive, for back at
headquarters the winter lull continued, marked at the moment by nothing more urgent than a circular to the army
requesting that dead animals lying around the camps be
buried to a depth of at least four feet.[7] But even in this official broadside observers expecting action might have seen an
omen. The weather was changing, and the notice about burying carcasses meant that spring temperatures were on their
way; that warriors, now as much intent on warming themselves as on fighting a war, soon would concentrate solely on
driving back the foe.

For a week before the messenger started on his trek, Betty
Van Lew kept him secluded in her home and forced him to
memorize certain data for General Butler—data too important
to set down on paper. Chief of these were the strength and
location of Rebel troops around Richmond. Also included was

advice on the best way to get into the city: make a feint on Petersburg, let Meade engage Lee on the Rappahannock, send 200 to 300 men and land them at White House on the other side of the city to attract attention, and then have 10,000 cavalry go up in the evening and rush upon it from the opposite direction next morning. But most important: Richmond could be taken more easily now than at any time since the start of the war.

In his mind Butler worked out a coordinated plan of attack, one that for some reason bore only slight resemblance to that advised by Betty Van Lew. She had urged an advance on Richmond from the west, supported by three diversionary movements—a feint at Petersburg, another along the Rapidan, and a third at White House, on the Pamunkey River to the east. Ben decided to dash on the city from Williamsburg and to dispense with all feints except that along the Rapidan. This action, he thought, should come first.

On the Rapidan the officer Butler had to deal with in Meade's absence was John Sedgwick, bachelor representative of the regular army. He was an addict of practical jokes and solitaire, yet a leader whose solemn manner sent chills down the spines of the rank and file; and he was also an individualist who at times verged on the ridiculous by adorning his head with a hat that one of his soldiers said looked like a small beehive of straw.[8] Butler's first message required one full day to get an answer, even though it carried the important announcement that 8000 of Lee's troops had gone to make an attack on New Berne, North Carolina. When the reply came, it was negative, and only by appealing to the White House did Butler finally get a promise of cooperation from Sedgwick.

On the afternoon before the day Sedgwick was to start moving, Chief Signal Officer L. B. Norton, stationed atop Pony Mountain, gave notice that he could see two columns of smoke rising from the Confederate lines, something he took to mean brush-burning. But all was quiet at the fords; he could make out hostile batteries still in position.

Next morning Sedgwick's troops marched briskly to the banks of the Rapidan. At 11:00 A.M. the artillery opened, lobbing shells over toward enemy fortifications on the hills beyond; and then an entire brigade, holding their muskets above their heads, waded into icy water up to their waists and crossed over to the opposite side. All was going well. Signal Officer J. C. Wiggins, looking down from Garnett's Mountain, saw the Union cavalry swing out at the flank and Rebel pickets fall back before it. At its front galloped Judson Kilpatrick, only a minor light in this expedition that Ben Butler was steering.

Wiggins watched until 4:30 P.M., when mists along the river blocked his view.

In the early afternoon Sedgwick wired Butler of his action and asked: "How are matters progressing with you?" The answer came back: "A movement commenced this morning at nine o'clock. Shall strike Sunday morning at five o'clock. Keep up demonstration after that time." [9]

Before midnight all but 150 of Sedgwick's men had waded back across the Rapidan, and those remaining forded it later when an enemy threat to close in became alarming. The thrust had resulted in 200 wounded, many seriously, and a few killed.

Meanwhile things were going well with Butler, or so he thought. His column—composed of 4000 infantry, 2200 cavalry, and two light batteries, led by his able assistant, Brigadier General Isaac J. Wistar, a handsome officer who had begun his war service as colonel of the old Seventy-first Regiment—swung out of Williamsburg by ten o'clock in the morning. It made good time and was well on its way to begin the attack on Richmond before another day dawned fully. Every detachment commander was carefully instructed on what was expected of him, and Wistar personally had seen to the distribution of maps, spikes, matches, and files. Each soldier had six days' rations and seventy rounds of ammunition, thirty of them on his back.

All afternoon the troops marched. Night came on, cloudy and rainy and densely thick and black, with the weary men still in motion, and, as they trudged along, cursing the mud and the February cold and the darkness, Confederate scouts lay in the woods along the roadside and listened.

By 2:30 A.M. the vanguard of cavalry reached Bottom's Bridge, within twelve miles of Richmond, and halted to wait until daylight before proceeding. But when the impenetrable blackness of night began to give way to a gray light in the east, riders feeling their way cautiously forward met with a surprise. Not for two months, since the dreaded winter weather had brought large-scale operations to a standstill, had this point been guarded by the Confederates. But it was heavily posted now, with three regiments of infantry, one of cavalry, and four batteries of artillery. These were ready to put up a terrific defense. Earthworks had been constructed, the bridge taken up, and fords above and below obstructed with felled trees. Persons living in the vicinity said that the Southerners at that point had known for sixteen hours that the Federals were coming.

At dawn the strength of the Rebels was tested by a detachment of the First New York Mounted Rifles, a picked company with picked horses. They charged in a great clattering thrust at one of the fords, men shouting hoarsely in the early-morning mists banking the Chickahominy, nervous horses rearing and screaming; and results were anything but encouraging. Nine men fell under the fire poured down by the Confederates. Sharply rebuffed, the Union horsemen scattered and retreated. Back to Wistar they went with news that somebody had slipped up somewhere, that this certainly was no sleepy outpost they had run up against on the other side of the stream.

Before noon the infantry Butler was sending to assist the cavalry at Bottom's Bridge, by marching forty miles in twenty-seven hours, got so close that Wistar began to think he might possibly run roughshod over the Confederates down at the ford. But what was the use? The enemy had given evidence of advance knowledge of Federal plans, so the main objective already was defeated. What would happen was obvious: the wily Rebels would march the Union prisoners in Richmond off in a body while the gates of the city were being stormed. So Wistar turned his column about and directed it toward New Kent Court House, moving hurriedly at first to escape the Gray horsemen who came charging up threateningly in the rear.

As the column proceeded homeward, Wistar began asking questions. Who had talked? Who had tipped off the enemy about the raid? A partial answer awaited him at Fortress Monroe. It came aboard a flag-of-truce steamer that had been up James River, and it was in the form of a single paragraph buried in the columns of that morning's Richmond *Examiner:*

"Some days since a report was obtained by authorities here from a Yankee deserter that the enemy was contemplating a raid in considerable force on Richmond. The report obtained consistence from a number of circumstances, and impressed the authorities to such a degree that a disposition of forces was made to anticipate the supposed designs of the enemy."

Armed with this tip from Confederate sources, the investigators back-tracked rapidly. Evidence pointed accusingly toward Fort Magruder, near Williamsburg, and in short order a private named Tom Abraham was hauled into custody. Evidence revealed that, while on sentinel duty from the One Hundred and Thirty-ninth New York, he had been swayed by easy talk and a bribe. These had come from Irishman William Boyle of the New York Mounted Rifles, held in close confinement on a charge of murder. In addition to allowing prisoner Boyle to escape, Abraham had acquainted him with the news that a large number of cavalry and infantry were being concentrated in an effort to take Richmond.[10]

So Butler had rung up another fiasco, and the men involved were once more back in their old quarters. There too was Kilpatrick, alert, restless, inspired with ideas about how success might have been achieved and itching to try his own hand at such an undertaking.

3

Opinion Divided

As KILPATRICK LEARNED, it was no problem to convince Abraham Lincoln that something should be done to relieve the plight of the Union soldiers held in Richmond. Stories of their starvation diet and cramped quarters continued to seep into official channels. Letters of protest, some crying out bitterly against government policy, came to Lincoln's desk. And then was added an inflammatory development: some of the much-discussed prisoners managed to gain their freedom, bringing firsthand accounts of what was going on behind the walls of Libby Prison.

This escape was made possible by a resolute band of fifteen valiant souls, headed by a thirty-three-year-old Pennsylvania colonel named Thomas E. Rose. For forty-two nights, while their fellow inmates slumbered on floors above, they pecked away at a sixty-five-foot tunnel, extending it entirely under and beyond one of Richmond's principal streets. Two nights after Butler's rebuff at Bottom's Bridge, 109 prisoners, Colonel Streight among them, crawled to freedom.

The tales these men told about Libby were shuttled to

Washington from points along their escape routes, and soon Lincoln became thoroughly convinced, despite Butler's fiasco, that a raid on Richmond would be worth all the risk involved. As he visualized it, such a venture would serve more than one purpose. Besides the release of prisoners still held in the dreadful war prisons of the city, copies of the amnesty proclamation he had issued the previous December could be distributed over a wide area along the raid route, especially among Rebel soldiers stationed on the Rapidan. This document offered full pardon to persons of Confederate sympathy, with certain exceptions, provided they took an oath of allegiance to the United States.[1] Still another function of the expedition would be to destroy enemy communications.[2]

One of Lincoln's first acts to get the second raid under way was to send a message through Major General Alfred Pleasonton, Cavalry Corps chief, for Judson Kilpatrick to report to the White House immediately. There was no explanation: it was simply a terse order from the President.

But Kilpatrick suspected what was in the wind as he rode away from the comfortable mansion serving as his headquarters. He had seen to it that Lincoln heard of his own scheme for getting into Richmond, and he had done all he could to make sure no person other than himself was chosen to carry it out.

At the White House Lincoln kept Kilpatrick only long enough to discuss briefly what was planned, and then sent him to the War Department. There the cavalry leader was directed to return to camp and to draft an outline of how he would go about making this successful dash on Richmond.

Kilpatrick already had most of the details of the daring venture in mind, so it took him but a short time to set them down on paper. The project he proposed was ambitious, and that was to be expected, for Judson himself was ambitious; he wanted to be governor of New Jersey and then President of the United States, and this mad ride into enemy territory might very well supply the impetus to start him along his shining path. Once given approval, he would ride forth with 4000 cavalry and six guns. Crossing the Rapidan at Ely's Ford, he would proceed to Spotsylvania Court House, where he would send out two detachments, one to cut telegraph lines and destroy the Virginia Central Railroad at or near Frederick's Hall, thus barring infantry reinforcements from Lee's army, and the other to tear up the Fredericksburg Railroad at or near Guiney's Station. Meanwhile, with the main force, he would move to Mount Carmel Church, cross the North Anna River, burn the railroad bridge three miles below, and proceed to Hanover Junction—provided Rebel troops stationed there were not too numerous. If his schedule worked as planned, he would be rejoined at Mount Carmel Church by the force sent to Guiney's. The other detachment, after striking Frederick's Hall, would proceed to Goochland Court House, cross the James River, and move along its south bank, destroying the canal, the arsenal at Bellona, and the Richmond & Danville and Richmond & Petersburg Railroads en route. The main force in the meantime would advance on the Confederate capital from Hanover Junction and make an attempt to release the prisoners, possibly with the aid of troops that Butler could send from West Point, a few miles away.

Whether or not success was gained at Richmond, the raiders would have no trouble escaping, for two routes of flight were open to them: one the direct path by which they would come, the other in the opposite direction, toward West Point, where they would seek temporary safety in Butler's lines. At any rate, just five days' rations for the men and one for the horses would be needed. He would take no wagons, only ambulances. Speed of execution was essential.

After outlining the details in his report, the young brigadier announced: "From the information I have but lately received, and from my thorough knowledge of the country, I am satisfied that this plan can be safely and successfully carried out." [8]

Soon after Kilpatrick returned from Washington, Pleasonton got orders to report to Meade's headquarters. There
the Cavalry Corps leader was asked his opinion of the proposed raid on Richmond. The question must have come to
him as a surprise, for he required some hours for deliberation
before answering, and when he replied he did so in writing. It
was a proposition he heartily disapproved. To him things
seemed to be getting out of hand. The idea of such an expedition should have come first of all from him, as commander
of cavalry. Certainly he—or at most Meade—should have been
the one to take it to the White House; some top officer rather
than a brigadier leading a division. This opinion caused him
to assess the venture with a stubbornness born of self-pride, an
obstinacy that would bring him disfavor with the War Department, even if its estimate of him had not already begun
to sour.

Pleasonton termed the plan emphatically "not feasible at
this time." [4] To begin with, he recalled the raid that had been
made by Stoneman on the Rebel capital during the Chancellorsville campaign the previous year, citing that it resulted
in a loss of 7000 horses, besides equipment and men, and the
only damage inflicted was easily repaired. Cutting the telegraph wires, he feared, would not block communications with
Richmond, and he also saw danger in the facilities the Confederates might have for defending the city while the armies
lay idle. Furthermore, he had information that the amnesty
proclamation already had been freely circulated in Virginia
and, even if it had not, such a matter could be attended to
without placing the responsibility on highly trained cavalry
prepared for battle action rather than behind-the-lines activity. Anyway, should they happen to get Lincoln's amnesty
offer, Union sympathizers in the state were so closely watched
they could not respond. Take a man at Howardsville: he had
secreted $160,000 in coin but had never been able to escape
with it.

For all his deliberation and careful assessment, Pleasonton's opinion was ignored.[5] This was because the pressure was on from the White House, from the commander-in-chief of all military forces, leaving little for the man in uniform to do to stop it.

Meanwhile Meade, who may not have been entirely in favor of the project, realized the situation and set the wheels in motion. The plan might work and, if so, it would be a master stroke. In fact, his latest information from Richmond was favorable. Sources considered reliable reported the city relatively defenseless, having within its boundaries only 3000 local militia, some field batteries, and a small body of horse. Moreover, Wade Hampton's division of cavalry, numbering a bare 1500, was the only part of Lee's army between Fredericksburg and the Rebel capital, and was at the moment too far away to be counted on for protection. It was Meade's opinion that, by a rapid and secret movement, Richmond might be carried by a *coup de main* and the prisoners released before reinforcements could be brought from either Lee or Petersburg.

The project began to develop. As early as the 18th, Kilpatrick got orders to send an officer to Washington to select horses for the projected expedition. These animals, it was cautioned, must be of the very best, well shod and able to take the strain of days and nights of hard, merciless riding.

4

Portents More Tangible Than Talk

For Nurse Cornelia Hancock, virtuous slave of the Army of the Potomac, camp routine quickly returned to drabness after the Washington's Birthday celebration. Scarcely two days passed before she was writing her sister: "There is nothing of importance here: the drums beat, the bugle sounds, the winds blow, the men groan—that is all." [1]

Cornelia's world was confined, largely by her own hand, to II Corps' Third Division hospital. There she put in a day that was noted for its lack of rest periods, and then at night, tired but happy in her work, she settled down to write letters and to keep score for the surgeons while they relaxed at cards. Now and then, bending over her pen, she heard snatches of conversation that made her think perhaps things were not as quiet as she supposed, at least not out beyond the boundaries of the hospital. Somebody said that II Corps was undergoing a thorough inspection. And then someone else observed that that could mean only one thing: a major move in the offing.

However, there were portents more tangible than talk. The omen of greatest significance was the presence of tall, blond

Ulric Dahlgren. Here was a young man dedicated to a successful culmination of the war. He had given a part of his body, his right leg, just three months after attaining the age of manhood, and that would seem quite enough. But not for this patriot. He had got into the war during the early months, when barely past his nineteenth birthday. And then his fighting ability, plus the influence of his father, had brought him favored attention and kept him constantly in the limelight.

Born in Pennsylvania and reared in Washington, where he spent many hours with his father in the ordnance department of the Navy Yard, Ulric was motherless at thirteen and out of school at sixteen. The war found him studying for the bar in a Philadelphia law office, but this ambition he quickly forsook when all the excitement began. Back in the national capital during the summer of '61, he took part in the early defense of the city as member of a detachment sent out from the Navy Yard. He was with this detachment when it was rushed off to answer a sudden emergency in the neighborhood of Harpers Ferry; and he came back from there alone, on a special assignment in quest of more ammunition. This was a fortunate mission for it brought Ulric into the presence of his father at a time when Admiral Dahlgren was seated in conversation with Lincoln and Secretary of War Stanton. The President had just written the Cabinet member that he would like to gratify a certain freakish desire expressed by the admiral—to have his son appointed a lieutenant in the army. Stanton complied when the young man appeared, appointing him aide-de-camp with rank of captain.

A short time later Ulric—called "Little Ully" in boyhood— was added to the staff of General Franz Sigel and he saw service up and down the Shenandoah Valley, on the Rappahannock, at Second Bull Run, and along the Washington defenses. He proved himself a good soldier, and in November '62, he was asked by Sigel to determine the Rebel strength at Fredericksburg, prior to the great battle fought there the following month. This he did with a small cavalry force, engaging in a little street fighting and hurrying away unharmed, mission fulfilled.[2] When the Federals pushed across at that point a few weeks later, Ulric was with the first troops sent to silence Rebel sharpshooters in the town.

Soon he was transferred to Hooker's staff for the Chancellorsville campaign. At Beverley Ford the next month he was hotly engaged, barely escaping capture when his horse went down wounded in three places. His status as a staffer remained unchanged when Meade took over on the way to Gettysburg, and he kept constantly busy, taking part in flank action and in the pursuit of Lee's army. Judson Kilpatrick was out there fighting too, and their paths finally crossed. At Boonsboro on July 6 they were together; and in scattered fighting along the streets, on their way out of town, Dahlgren was shot in the foot.[3] He kept to his saddle, too proud to yield to what he considered a minor wound, but loss of blood soon put him out of action. Three days later he was brought to his father's home in Washington on a litter, and in a matter of hours his leg was amputated below the knee. Then came a period of slow convalescence.

While he lay abed, many prominent officials came to see him, among them Lincoln, Hooker, and Stanton. The Secretary of War was there to tell him he had been jumped to the rank of colonel.

These days of idleness gave the young man an opportunity to engage in serious thinking; and some of his reflections he revealed in letters. "Often while lying down in my room," he wrote an aunt, "I think over what I have seen and what has taken place since I first came home wounded. It seems like a dream and puzzles me to think of 'Death' and wonder what it is." And again: "How little we know who will go next." [4]

By mid-October, Dahlgren was able to move about with the aid of crutches. He was impatient to get back into the field of action, and sometimes at night he visited the camps around Washington, to sit and talk and discuss with others what was going on at the front.[5] In November he went to South Carolina to visit his father and to watch a fleet in action. His stay extended to the following January. Only a few hours after his return to Washington, he heard of Kilpatrick's wild scheme to storm Richmond. The temptation was too great for his young blood. Backed by the good connections of an admiral's son, he hurried away to have a part in it.

At Stevensburg, where he arrived by train with the Washington's Birthday celebrants, Dahlgren met with an immediate welcome. Kilpatrick was looking for a man of his type, a fearless leader who would push on in the face of any adversity, ready to fight and determined to win. And then there was the matter of prestige! A son of Admiral Dahlgren would bring renown to any expedition.

Thus the two came together, a young brigadier and a young colonel. But they were not complements to each other. Dahlgren possessed a spotless record, both personal and military; but people had their misgivings about Kilpatrick. He was not by any means what might be termed the perfect soldier.[6] Just turned twenty-eight, a graduate of West Point, of high intellect and all that, yes; but not a man of refinement or of high morals.[7] He was fiery and tempestuous and at times licentious, a gifted orator, a practical joker, and an amateur actor so enamored of theatrics that he one day would write a full-fledged melodrama. But the battlefield was the stage on which he would do his greatest acting.

As an army man, he liked the show and the clatter-bang of the cavalry. Always, whether in camp or on the march, he was ambitious, restless, running over with energy. Yet there was something in his make-up that verged on the ridiculous, and now and then he acted in such a way that no less a person than General William Tecumseh Sherman called him "a hell of a damned fool." [8] Clothed in a rakish manner, below medium height, small of body, with reddish-sandy hair, gingery sidewhiskers, and a hawklike face, he was so odd in appearance that one of his fellow officers declared, "It is hard to look at him without laughing." [9]

But the greatest fault to be found with Kilpatrick was the ruthless manner in which he operated, without regard for men or horses. Thus he won his nickname—"Kilcavalry." [10] And though months had passed since the bloody fighting at Gettysburg, men in the ranks still talked about the way he had driven poor Elon Farnsworth to his death. There were witnesses close enough to hear Farnsworth's protest when Kilpatrick ordered him to charge against Rebels hidden behind stone walls. Then from Kilpatrick: "If you are afraid to lead this charge, I will lead it." The gallant young man, just recently made brigadier, rose in his stirrups and shouted, "Take that back!" Judson took it back, and his junior officer rode away to his slaughter, muttering over his shoulder, "I will obey your orders." [11]

That sort of rashness on the part of a leader, coupled with the fact that he was known to have lost his head when beset with self-invited perils, made Kilpatrick a man in whom it was difficult to have complete confidence. [12]

February 26, the fourth day after the birthday ball, found Meade waiting with everything in readiness for the hour when the column would depart. As the project got under way, his army would be generally active; but all movements, with one exception, would be designed to confuse the enemy. Sedgwick would begin the operations. Two regiments of his VI Corps would start from their camp on Saturday, in time to reach Madison Court House by Sunday evening. With them they would take six days' rations, forty rounds of ammunition per man, three batteries, ambulances, entrenching tools, and hospital and headquarters wagons. "Secrecy is essential to success," Sedgwick was cautioned, but these words were mockery. With such an array of vehicles, there could be no reason to worry much about whether the enemy discovered the movement.

At Madison, Sedgwick was to stand by as cover and support for a cavalry operation led by the young cavalry brigadier, blond, wavy-haired George Custer, an officer as much given to flashy dress as the Rebel leader, Jeb Stuart. Custer's column, 1500 strong, would arrive after dark Sunday and move on at two o'clock next morning. According to written orders, they would have no specific objective. They would merely ride as near Charlottesville as they could safely get, keeping in mind a possibility that the enemy might try to intercept them. If they were able, they would burn the bridge across the Rivanna River; otherwise, they would simply turn about and come on back to Madison. Obviously, as outlined at headquarters, the entire movement was a feint.

Another bit of deception was to precede Custer's departure: in broad daylight Sunday morning, parts of III Army Corps, commanded by Major General David B. Birney, were to march through Culpeper from Brandy Station and take the road to James City, all in plain sight of the Rebel signal station on Clark's Mountain. At its destination it would go into camp and wait as a reserve to Sedgwick's troops.

Great secrecy was maintained in the preparation of Kilpatrick's orders, a rather odd development in view of the general knowledge in and out of the camps at Brandy Station that the raid was coming. New York newspapers, even before all the men who were to take part had been selected, were preparing stories and maps and getting ready to broadcast the news while the thrust was still in progress. One of Meade's staff sarcastically reflected that "a secret expedition with us is got up like a picnic, with everybody blabbing and yelping." [13] As for the enemy, General Lee had anticipated the attempt on Richmond since November. Scouts had brought him reports that indicated to his experienced military eye that

Meade hoped to strike at the Confederate capital; and so well could the Rebel commander-in-chief size up the situation at hand that he was even able to pinpoint the ford on the Rapidan over which it would come.[14] But Meade ignored all this— if he knew it. As far as he was concerned, the projected raid was still known only to the military. For instance, Pennington's battery of light artillery was directed at four o'clock Friday afternoon to report to Kilpatrick. "The movement of the battery should be made so as to escape the observation of the enemy, and so far as practicable that of our army," read the orders.[15]

Kilpatrick got his instructions on Saturday: "You will move with the utmost expedition possible on the shortest route past the enemy's right flank to Richmond, and by this rapid march endeavor to effect an entrance into that city and liberate our prisoners now held there and in that immediate vicinity." [16] The orders came first from Pleasonton and were repeated next day by Meade. In them official authority was given for Dahlgren to take part. He was expected to "render valuable assistance from his knowledge of the country and his well-known gallantry, intelligence, and energy." [17]

The movement was to begin the night of the 28th. Four thousand men would be provided for the expedition, to be supported by a wholesale diversion in the opposite direction. But the manner in which his mission was to be executed was left entirely up to him. "I am directed by the major-general commanding," wrote the chief of staff, "to say that no detailed instructions are given you, since the plan of your operations has been proposed by yourself, with the sanction of the President and the Secretary of War, and has been so far adopted by him that he considers success possible with secrecy, good management, and the utmost expedition." [18]

Thus the responsibility was Kilpatrick's. Once he left his base, the fate of himself and his men was in his own hands. It would seem he had nothing to worry about: the officers

who outranked him were confident of success. Even Pleasonton, lone avowed foe of the plan, would appear to be in
this group. In a simple statement to headquarters he disposed
of the sole enemy element known to be between the Confederate troops stationed along the Rapidan and those in Richmond: "Kilpatrick can easily handle Hampton without
assistance." [19]

While preparations for the raid proceeded, Ulric Dahlgren
sent out some letters. To an aunt in Washington, D.C., Mrs.
M. M. Dahlgren, he wrote: "I have written a letter to Father.
When it comes, keep it until you hear whether we succeed
in our raid or not. If I do not return, then give it to him. We
will start soon, and, I think, will succeed, and, if so, it will
be the grandest thing on record. I have not the slightest fear
about not returning, but we can't always tell, so don't be
uneasy *nor say a word to anyone.*" [20]

In the letter to his father he said: "I have not returned to
the fleet because there is a grand raid to be made and I am to
have a very important command. If successful it would be
the grandest thing on record and if it fails many of us will
'go up.' I may be captured or I may be 'tumbled over,' but
it is an undertaking that if I was not in it I should be ashamed
to show my face again, with such an important command.
I am afraid to mention it for fear this letter might fall into
the wrong hands before reaching you. I find that I can stand
the service perfectly well without my leg. I think we will
be successful although a desperate undertaking. Aunt Patty
can tell you when you return. I will write you more fully
when we return—if we do not return there is no better place
to 'give up the Ghost.' "

Meade, apparently still not too certain of the wisdom of
his "grand raid" and trying to solidify conviction of its justification, also was writing. In a letter to his wife he revealed:
"I have been a great deal occupied with an attempt I am
about making, to send a force of cavalry into Richmond to

liberate our prisoners. The undertaking is a desperate one, but the anxiety and distress of the public and the authorities at Washington is so great that it seems to demand running great risks for the chances of success." [21]

5

The Path of Destiny

Before it was taken over as a campsite by the Army of the Potomac, Stevensburg was a tiny, ambitious hamlet on the road to Richmond. It had a carefully laid network of streets and it was blessed with rare landscape features, including the faint line of the Blue Ridge in the distance, which had induced Thomas Jefferson to consider the community as a site for his aristocratic University of Virginia.

Now, across the countryside as far as human eye could see, toward Brandy Station and Culpeper, the county seat, and south across the Rapidan where the Confederates lay, flickered a maze of campfires. They burned on land that had been fought over time and again, by big armies and by scattered bands too small to have won a place in the records. Houses not actually reduced to ashes looked worse than those that had, for generally their windows were without sashes, doors missing, and walls stripped of boards. Acres of stumps showed where once good timber had stood. On all sides marks of old camps were plainly visible—burnt spots where the fires had been, trenches bordering tent sites, old bones, tin pots, frag-

39

ments of shell, skeletons of horses and mules, and here and there a little ridge of earth set off by a piece of plank on which had been scribbled a name.[1] Before darkness set in—and even afterward, some folks believed—the air above was crossed and recrossed by the constant and haunting flights of buzzards and crows.

Stevensburg lay close to the Rapidan, a quiet little stream winding on down to join the Rappahannock near Fredericksburg—quiet until storms swelled it over its banks. To the west, separated by even a shorter stretch of field, was Pony Mountain.[2] In 1864 it was a forested bulwark that provided altitude for the nearest of the Union signal stations, and from its crest off to the south could be viewed other nearby mountains—Stony, the closest; Clark's, Rebel lookout; and, to the southwest, in the direction of the towering Blue Ridge, the more imposing outline of Garnett's.

Up there on Pony, flags waved or lights blinked at all hours as signalmen coded their messages, bits of information they were able to pick up by their own observation or from intercepted communication of the Confederates. "A large campfire seen today in Swift Run Gap." . . . "Woods on fire on hill near Orange C. H." . . . "All quiet during the night."

In this setting the usual Sunday quiet of February 28 was broken by an unusual undercurrent of activity. It had gone on throughout the night, confined to the camps and not extending as far as the outposts. Even the weather appeared to be cooperating with the project at hand. At dawn a smoky haze lay over the land, blocking observation and, as the hours advanced, maintaining its density and shutting off the rays of the sun until late afternoon. This screen laid down by the elements brought almost complete isolation to Pony Mountain, especially to the promontory on which perched faithful Signal Officer Jedediah C. Paine. No matter how carefully he listened and searched the surrounding terrain, using a pair of heavy field glasses, the report he finally came up with was routine: except for a few picket shots due west, no firing had been heard since bedtime the night before.

Back of the subdued bustle, Meade's complicated screening action was developing bit by bit. Sedgwick had departed on Saturday, without obvious effort to conceal the movement, and now Birney's troops were on their way through Culpeper. Custer would follow in equally conspicuous fashion, his horses sloshing through the mud and making enough noise to be heard all the way up the slopes of Pony.

But actually, around the Federal camps, there was little concern over what Sedgwick and Birney were doing and much interest in what was going on in the neighborhood of the Rapidan. Noticeable for days had been a siege of preparation. Missing equipment was replaced and horses were carefully checked for shoeing, bolstering the rumor that there was more action imminent than just the thrust toward Madison Court House. This was borne out more clearly when preparations were noticed to have increased rather than abated long after Sedgwick's and even Custer's troops had left camp. For hours fragments of various cavalry units, all well mounted, could be seen shifting from point to point. The first transfer of these units had begun the night of the 27th, and here, hours later, men and horses still were standing by waiting to get under way—toward whatever goal was in store.

At the start of things an aide stalked importantly down the long array of tents set up for the Seventh Michigan Volunteer Cavalry and delivered an order in front of Colonel Allyne Litchfield's quarters: "Report your regiment at General Kilpatrick's headquarters promptly at sundown." [3] Bill Lee, acting adjutant, marched the unit away in compliance, only to wind up waiting in a bedlam of artillery, ambulances, and army wagons, the last of which, it was whispered, were filled with vast supplies of ammunition, powder, and turpentine.

The Seventeenth Pennsylvania Cavalry, camped near Culpeper, got orders to have 200 of its best men and horses report in light marching order to General Thomas C. Devin. Major W. H. Spera, assigned to command the detail, marched it off as directed and wound up in front of a puzzled Devin. The general said he had no idea what the Pennsylvanians were supposed to do; Spera had better go see the CO of the Sixth New York Cavalry detachment. This officer, Major William P. Hall, had just received orders to report to First Division headquarters, so the combined forces stomped away in that direction, only to be met by the same confusion. All anybody knew was that the point of assembly was Stevensburg. By that time the cavalrymen were pretty well convinced that what they were facing was a night ride. But when Hall rode up to the spacious old mansion in which Kilpatrick had spread his papers, he was directed to "go into camp and make yourselves comfortable." [4] In the life of a soldier, some things failed to make sense, and this was one.

All through the camps could be noticed this apparent lack of logic. The colonel of the Fifth Michigan Cavalry sent for Sam Harris, one of his most trusted lieutenants. "Take twenty-five men from Company K of our regiment," he ordered, "and report by midnight to Colonel Ulric Dahlgren at Stevensburg." Harris was dumfounded: K was not his responsibility.

"How about taking my company?" he asked.

"No. Take K. I want you to get some fighting out of them."

Sam went away shaking his head, and soon his detail wound up in a massed body of men from the Second and Fifth New York, First Vermont, and Fifth Michigan, all veteran cavalry.[5]

The shifting of units kept up through most of the 28th. At one period an order was brought from Kilpatrick's mansion: if any trooper or horse was not in condition for a long march, replacements should be made at once. Here and there men fell aside. Major Hall weeded out two from the Seventeenth Pennsylvania and filled the gaps.

Later a message was sent off by well-guarded courier to Major General G. K. Warren, whose II Corps was scattered along the Rapidan. It told him Kilpatrick would move after dark. It also warned that a brigade of Rebel cavalry had been noticed at Morton's Ford, thus requiring "more than usual vigilance" on the part of Union infantry stationed at that point.[6]

Late in the day rations were issued. Each man received enough hard bread, sugar, coffee, and salt to last three days.[7] But there was an obvious absence of meat. "This looks extremely raidish," observed an officer who prided himself on his powers of observation.[8]

There was much excitement, and everyone seemed in good humor. It had long been observed that nothing delighted a cavalryman more than prospect of active duty. "It is easier to get a trooper or even a hundred for a raid than to get one to groom an extra horse," commented a veteran trooper.[9]

Meanwhile all activities seemed to be going according to schedule. At two o'clock in the afternoon Sedgwick sent back a report. He already had pushed a brigade and battery into Madison Court House without resistance, and was standing by, bothered only by haze, which prevented his opening communications with the signal officer sent to Thoroughfare Mountain. Nearer Stevensburg, Custer, with 1500 cavalrymen, was on his way. He had left Pony at the very moment Sedgwick was preparing his report, and by 6:00 P.M. they would be together.

Fifteen minutes after the hour of six a confidential dispatch went out from Meade's headquarters. It was directed to Kilpatrick, and it gave the cavalry leader instructions he already had received in more detail the day before: "The major general commanding directs that you move tonight." [10]

Kilpatrick had not waited for anything as formal as a confidential dispatch. The orders he received on Saturday were to him quite enough, and fully explicit. Thus on the hour of six o'clock, even before Meade's headquarters sent the last directive, 500 men [11] swung out under command of the one-legged, blond-haired Dahlgren, a youthful leader satisfied in his own mind he was following the path of destiny.[12] Toward Ely's Ford they moved, each armed with a Spencer, Sharps, or Burnside carbine and two Colt army pistols. In the band were troopers from the First Maine, First Vermont, Fifth Michigan, and Second and Fifth New York Volunteer Cavalry, all hand-picked. Behind them, in sixty minutes, would come a long column of better than 3000 men under Kilpatrick, all similarly armed, all moving rapidly in the moonlight and braced for hours in the saddle.[13]

6

Hours of Darkness

As these troopers carrying Lincoln's hope for release of the prisoners in Richmond moved toward Ely's Ford, the haze that blanketed the land early in the day had disappeared. But in the distance to the west traces of it still were visible. Now shaken down into a white fog bank, it tarried in the moon's glow along the slopes of the mountains, ghostlike and unmoving and apparently harmless. But Union intelligence officers cast worried glances toward the westward slopes: no matter how innocent the fog might appear, it was enough to block out signal stations toward the Blue Ridge.[1]

Outside the range of the fog, around Stevensburg and off along the Rapidan, the countryside sprawled under a beautiful night. Joseph Gloskoski, Kilpatrick's signal officer, was so moved by it as to write in prose uncommon to military report: "Myriads of stars twinkled in heaven, looking at us as if in wonder why should we break the laws of God and wander at night instead of seeking repose and sleep. The moon threw its silvery light upon Rapidan waters when we forded it, and it seemed as if the Almighty Judge was looking silently upon our doings."[2]

45

At midnight Kilpatrick's column began fording the Rapidan.[3] Shortly before the troopers up front reached the stream, horsemen could be heard moving toward them out of the sweep of moonlight. Challenges quickly were exchanged, and soon twenty-three of Dahlgren's men came riding from the gloom, establishing first contact between the two cooperating forces. With them rode seventeen prisoners—a captain, a lieutenant, and fifteen privates—total strength of the Rebel picket on duty at Ely's Ford. They had been rounded up without a shot, a perfect example of the stealth with which Kilpatrick hoped to begin—and to continue—the raid.[4]

This capture was a tribute to Martin E. Hogan, nineteen-year-old Irish scout ruled by a yen for the daring.[5] The mission had no terrors for him. He was just back from the Rapidan. For days he had been riding through Confederate territory, and he knew the lay of the land. At the start of things back at Stevensburg, he had been stationed at the head of the column, a wise move, for at the right moment he adroitly led a detail of forty men across the stream, above Ely's Ford, and brought it in upon the rear of the picket.[6] It was just eleven o'clock when the first barrier on the road to Richmond thus was eliminated. And from the ease with which it was done, the raiders surmised that the enemy so far had no suspicion of what was happening.

Hogan was not the only guide riding with Dahlgren. Farther back in the column, unobtrusive and silent, was a Negro freedman, a bricklayer named Martin Robinson. At one time he had been a slave of the David Mimms family of Goochland Court House, and his present home was just twelve miles away, in the vicinity of Contention, a hamlet near Jude's Ferry, a point on the James River fordable except in time of freshet. It was there that local farmers and others crossed to reach Centre Hill in Powhatan County; and it was because of his knowledge of the area that Martin's presence was so important to Dahlgren.[7] He had been sent through the

Provost-Marshal General's Office, bringing the endorsement of an officer so convinced of the Negro's value that he supplied him with a private riding horse: "At the last moment I have found the man . . . ; well acquainted with the James River from Richmond up. . . . Question him five minutes and you will know him the very man you want." [8] This message to Dahlgren had a notation on the margin: "He crossed at Rapidan last night, and has late information."

When the ford had been cleared, Dahlgren, his crutch strapped to the side of his saddle, rode to the head of the column and gave a quick kick with the spur on his left foot. From there on speed was essential. Their next destination: Spotsylvania Court House, a little better than twelve miles away.

While the operations were under way at the ford, Dahlgren would have been better off had he devoted more attention to what was going on at the rear, for his approach was not unnoticed. At one point on the route from Stevensburg, two Confederates picked up the trail. These alert warriors were Hugh Henderson Scott and Dan Topping, scouts for the Rebel cavalry leader, Wade Hampton. Starting from Hamilton's Crossing near Fredericksburg, they had paddled over the Rappahannock on logs and stolen westward until they found their path blocked by Union horsemen. Without hesitating, they worked to the rear of the column and there captured two stragglers, conducting them deep into the woods before riding off on their horses. When the Federals came out on the opposite side of the ford, the two intruders faded into the mingling throng. Thus they continued, trotting along elbow to elbow with their enemies until they were able to veer off unseen and strike for Hampton's headquarters.[9]

Kilpatrick, behind Dahlgren by an hour's ride, was satisfied with the progress both columns were making. At one o'clock in the morning, while his men were crossing the ford in good order, talking soothingly to their horses before coaxing them down into the cold waters, he sent off a report to Lieutenant Colonel C. Ross Smith, Cavalry Corps chief of staff. "It was a complete surprise," he said of the picket-post capture. "No alarm has been given. The enemy does not anticipate our movement." [10] At that moment Dahlgren was at Chancellorsville, riding through fields scarred by the battle that had taken place there not quite a year past.

The New York *Tribune*'s correspondent recorded a subsequent Kilpatrick report that failed to show up in *Official Records*. According to this newsman, it was sent to General Pleasonton at eleven o'clock in the morning, told of the successful passage at Ely's Ford, and concluded: "Twenty miles nearer Richmond, and all right. Will double my bet of $5,000 that I enter Richmond." [11]

Before daylight Kilpatrick's column also was passing over the Chancellorsville battlefield. Every man was cautioned not to strike a light, for off in the darkness toward the northeast, in the vicinity of Fredericksburg, enemy picket fires were burning.

As they rode on through low, heavily wooded country, an occasional anxious eye was cast toward the heavens. Cloud banks had begun to form in the fading moonlight, and one of the weatherwise said that such dark masses betokened rain. Kilpatrick glanced at them with nervous concern. "Let the storm hold off twenty-four hours, and I won't care," he remarked prayerfully.[12]

The main column came into Spotsylvania Court House at eight o'clock in the morning, happy, hungry, and defiant. Along the roadside near the community an aged woman, broom in hand, was trying frantically to herd a flock of geese out of sight of the advancing horsemen, but the precaution had been delayed too long. Enthusiastically, like schoolboys at play, the Seventeenth Pennsylvania Cavalry came thundering down with sabers drawn, shouting and slashing and full of fun. In they charged, and one after another the goose heads rolled.

The woman, ignoring her years, struck back, her voice a shrill discord above the laughter of the men. From the safety of his saddle Captain L. B. Kurtz looked down at her and smilingly remarked, "Madam, these Yankees are hell on poultry." The remark stirred her fury, and she aimed at him a wide and futile sweep of her broom, after which, exhausted by frantic effort in a losing cause, she backed into her yard and slammed the gate. Then she shouted, "You ought to be ashamed of yo'-selves, coming here and destroying our things! You nothin' but nasty, dirty Yankees!" [13]

Everywhere along their route the raiders were impressed by the Sunday-like stillness, the large number of dilapidated and deserted dwellings, the ruined churches, standing with windows out and doors ajar. Fields and workshops were abandoned. Farms were neglected. People were ragged, dejected, uncouth. Men and boys were rarely encountered. One newspaper correspondent summed up the picture by saying that everything indicated "a condition of affairs which nothing but civil war could produce." [14]

While Kilpatrick's column was riding through Spotsylvania, Dahlgren's men were gathered on the roadside miles ahead, enjoying a fifteen-minute halt to feed their horses. On through the night they had pushed, for their youthful leader, despite his peg leg and tender stump, was enjoying himself immensely. Now, when his troopers climbed back to their saddles, he delayed the departure long enough to examine them more closely by daylight. Twice along the front of the column he rode, staring at each man. One officer who was present recorded: "Many had never seen him before. His appearance, however, gave general satisfaction, and expressions of confidence were heard all around." [15]

Two miles past Spotsylvania, Dahlgren's route swung to the right, in the direction of Frederick's Hall Station on the Virginia Central Railroad.[16] This turn-off was the point at which he parted paths with the main body. From there on he would be on his own, until the two forces met again—this time, if things developed as planned, while they stormed through the streets of Richmond.

Kilpatrick had carefully laid out the routes of advance: Dahlgren would swing wide, cross the James at a point above Goochland Court House, and come into Richmond from the south; while the other column, moving more slowly, would go directly toward the Confederate capital by way of Beaver Dam Station, Ground Squirrel Bridge, and Brook Turnpike. It was hoped that both would be in striking position by ten o'clock on the morning of March 1.

After passing through Spotsylvania, Kilpatrick continued his march a mile or more until the column had crossed Po River. There he halted to feed. When the ride was resumed, it would be directly toward Mount Pleasant, Chilesburg, and Beaver Dam Station. But a part of the troops, a small band under Captain Ted Boice, Fifth New York Cavalry, would swing off to the left to destroy the Richmond, Fredericksburg & Potomac Railroad at Guiney's. During the night the telegraph wires along both that line and the Virginia Central had been cut by scouts, to make sure no word of their approach was flashed to Richmond.

The stop near the Po lasted only long enough to brew a cup of coffee. This was not because of any scarcity of food: from almost every saddle hung a chicken, goose, ham, or side of meat, all purloined along the road. Sight of the indiscriminate larder stirred comment from Teddy Campbell of the Seventeenth Pennsylvania's Company I: "This is one of old Abe's jokes—plenty of rations, but no time to eat them." [17]

While the nearly 4000 chosen horsemen rode eastward, General Meade waited back at headquarters near Brandy Station for some report of their progress. At ten o'clock in the morning he sent off a message to Chief of Staff Halleck in Washington, giving the first official notice that the raid was under way: "A cavalry expedition left last evening with the intention of attempting to carry Richmond by a *coup de main*, General Kilpatrick in command. If successful, expects to be there by tomorrow P.M., March 1, and may the next day be in the vicinity of General Butler's outposts and pickets. Will you please notify that officer, that his advanced posts may be warned?" [18] This report was in the Union capital an hour later, and it was immediately relayed to Butler, from whom came a reply that 2000 infantry, 1000 cavalry, and a battery would be sent to New Kent Court House by three o'clock Wednesday afternoon "to aid in case of disaster, to receive prisoners, or to cover retreat." [19]

Dahlgren in the meantime had hurried on toward Frederick's Hall, where he had information that heavy guns from the Confederate Second Corps were parked. At eleven o'clock in the morning he drew up within three quarters of a mile of the place to intercept a Confederate court-martial then in progress in an empty house beside the road. It was a rich haul —a lieutenant colonel, three captains, four lieutenants, and several privates.[20]

There were other prisoners to keep them company. Along the way the column had rounded up sixteen artillerymen. The two groups were combined and a barrage of questions aimed at them. The object: to learn what to expect at Frederick's Hall.

One of the artillery soldiers, John Hurry of the First Maryland Battery, appeared to Dahlgren to be none too bright, so he was led off to the side—"Come, John, we got things to talk about"—for some special questioning. John was willing enough to talk.

"What artillery?" he repeated in answer to the first question. "They got lots of it, and every regiment guarded by five regiments of cavalry. What's more, they done split up one regiment into battalions of sharpshooters. That's for special guard duty."

"I believe you're lying," said one of his questioners.

Hurry turned and pointed toward the station. "See that building yonder? That's brigade headquarters, and behind that hill over there where you see the smoke rising is the camp. Go on—try to capture it, so I can git free."

"If you're lying, you'll be shot," said the Federal.

Hurry ignored the remark.

At that moment an old Negro was brought up and identified as a slave from a nearby plantation.

"How many soldiers are stationed at Frederick's Hall?" asked Dahlgren.

"Fo' de Lawd, boss, ain't no tellin'. But dar's a heap uv 'em," the Negro replied.

"What kind—infantry or artillery?"

"Lawd bless yo' soul, boss, I don't know what dey is. But dar's a heap uv 'em."

"Do they have big guns or little guns?"

"Dey got bof." [21]

Another Negro, younger and more flashily dressed, was brought into the circle. "Is there any infantry at Frederick's Hall?" he was asked.

"Yassuh, dere sho is infanry dere," he replied without hesitation.

"How do you know?"

" 'Cause I done seen 'em—seen 'em wif my own eyes."

"How do you know they are infantry?"

" 'Cause. Ain't no trubble t' tell infanry. Dem's de ones wif de stickers on de ends o' dere guns, ain't dey?"

Others, including the officers from the court-martial, were questioned. Their replies all gave pretty much the same picture—one of strength. They told of three different camps at the station, each with eight batteries of artillery, in all about ninety-six guns. Near at hand, they said, was a regiment of infantry, while each camp was equipped with a battalion of sharpshooters.

Dahlgren listened and was swayed by caution: this was the

Brigadier General Judson Kilpatrick, leader of the Federal Army's Third Division, stands in full regalia before a tent at his headquarters on the Rapidan. Photograph taken late in the winter of 1864, just before Kilpatrick started his raid on Richmond.

Colonel Ulric Dahlgren as he appeared before he lost his leg in the Gettysburg campaign.

Pen-and-ink sketch of Kilpatrick's camp made shortly before the raid
on Richmond.

Two soldiers from Kilpatrick's cavalry sitting in the camp street of the billet at Stevensburg.

A colonel before his elaborate quarters, Army of the Potomac headquarters, winter of 1864.

Winter quarters of scouts and guides employed by Federal troops along the Rapidan.

Winter headquarters of General Marsena R. Patrick, near Brandy Station.

Billet occupied by the Signal Corps attached to Meade's army as it lay along the Rapidan.

Ulric Dahlgren pictured standing among a group of distinguished officers during his service on General Meade's staff. The others, *left to right*: Major Ludlow, who commanded the colored brigade that dug the Dutch Gap Canal on the James River; Lieutenant Colonel Dickinson, assistant adjutant general to General Hooker; Count von Zeppelin, observer from the Prussian Army, later to become famous for his dirigibles; and Lieutenant Rosencranz, General McClellan's personal aide-de-camp.

An advanced report of the raid, pieced together by a correspondent at Meade's headquarters and published while the raiders were on their way back to camp.

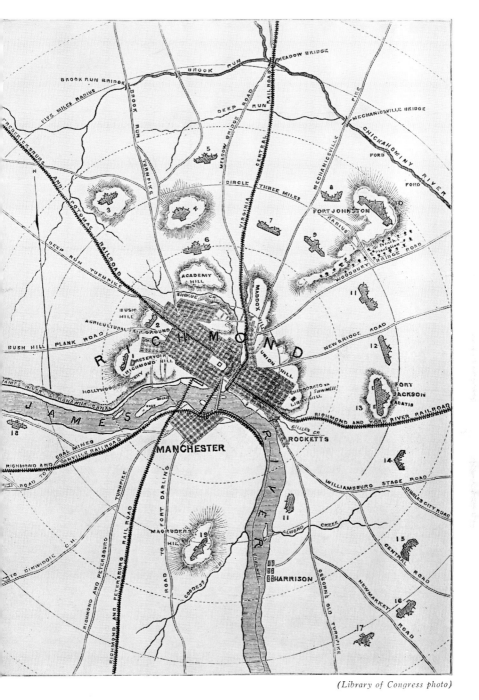

The fortifications around Richmond, including the earthworks along Brook Turnpike, that enabled the besieged Confederates to turn back Kilpatrick's troopers.

Scene by Waud, famous Civil War artist, depicting Scout Martin E. Hogan as he waded back across the Rapidan to report to Kilpatrick that he had wiped out the Confederate guard at Ely's Ford.

View of Libby Prison from across Twentieth Street, looking toward the canal and river.

View of Libby Prison from the river side, with Kanawha Canal
in foreground. The escape of Rose and his men was effected
through door of small building at the far right.

Pen-and-ink sketch of Belle Isle from the Richmond side of James
River.

Belle Isle as pictured in *The Photographic History of the Civil War*. The tall figure in foreground is Major Thomas P. Turner, commandant of Belle Isle and Libby Prison. Tents at the river's edge belong to guards. On the hill in the background is the column-fronted Capitol building of the Confederacy.

(Library of Congress photo)

(Library of Congress photo)

A fanciful conception of Dahlgren's men charging the Confederate irregulars at the outskirts of Richmond.

(Library of Congress photo)

The scene at Dahlgren's Corner, name given the spot where the young colonel fell, as it appeared in horse-and-buggy days.

(Library of Congress photo)

Crossed flags mark the grave of Colonel Ulric Dahlgren in North Hill Cemetery, Philadelphia.

No. CCCLXXVI.

FRENCH'S STANDARD DRAMA.

𝕿𝖍𝖊 𝕬𝖈𝖙𝖎𝖓𝖌 𝕰𝖉𝖎𝖙𝖎𝖔𝖓.

"ALLATOONA,"

An Historical and Military

𝕯𝖗𝖆𝖒𝖆

IN FIVE ACTS,

BY

MAJOR-GENERAL JUDSON KILPATRICK,

AND

J. OWEN MOORE, ESQ.

Author of "STRIFE" and "TEMPTED."

NEW YORK:	LONDON:
Samuel French & Son,	Samuel French,
PUBLISHERS,	PUBLISHER,
122 NASSAU STREET.	89 STRAND.

Title page of Judson Kilpatrick's five-act drama, *Allatoona*, later produced in the old Rialto Theater in Hoboken, N. J.

wrong end of the raid to be taking foolish chances. So, on the strength of what he was able to get out of the prisoners, he decided against attack. Thus was saved for the South the entire artillery of the Second Corps. The guns, as reported, were parked for the winter and were protected by only a handful of sharpshooters.[22]

But the greatest miss during the raid was controlled by fate rather than by human decision. Only a short while before Dahlgren's troopers reached Frederick's Hall, a train passed. On board, unaware of the nearness of enemy riders, was General Lee, hurrying back to Orange Court House from the conferences at Richmond. His capture would have been a fatal blow to the Army of Northern Virginia. Many of its members were fighting, at that stage of the war, perhaps more for their leader, a tangible hero admired by all, than for their cause, an intangible principle not entirely clear to many.[23]

After deciding against attack, Dahlgren turned off on a wide circuit, following farm roads in the direction of Bumpass Station, and struck the railroad south of Frederick's Hall at Gunnell's Crossing. There he ordered his men down from their saddles for a busy period of destruction. And while they went about it, tearing up rails and heating them on huge bonfires made from the seasoned wood of the ties, a train appeared from the west. It chugged into view and stopped, its engineer alarmed by the smoke ahead. For a while it waited uncertainly and then backed hastily out of sight. The black clouds pouring from its potbellied stack sank slowly to earth, another omen to the weatherwise that some form of precipitation was on its way.[24]

By this time Confederate General Wade Hampton was well aware that the Federals were staging a raid. First the two scouts from Ely's Ford, Scott and Topping, had appeared; then Sergeant Shadbourne, another of his spies. The sergeant also had been on the road between the ford and Stevensburg the night before and had watched the blue-clad troops ride past in the moonlight. The movement appeared to be general, he said, and, in preparation for it, sutlers and women had been moved to the rear.[25] Hampton promptly sent this information to Jeb Stuart; an hour and a half later he added that a Yankee cavalry brigade was en route to the Virginia Central Railroad.

But no reply came from Stuart, so Hampton proceeded to organize resistance without direction from Cavalry Corps headquarters. Few troops were available to him. Near at hand were 253 members of the First North Carolina Cavalry, fifty-three of the Second, and two guns from Hart's battery. These were directed to move southward along the R. F. & P., and an order was sent to Colonel Bradley Johnson's Maryland brigade to join them from Taylorsville.[26]

Kilpatrick meanwhile was striking toward Beaver Dam, a wood station on the Virginia Central. Now that the two commands were following separate routes, Joseph Gloskoski, the signal officer, was instructed to maintain some sort of contact with Dahlgren. This Dahlgren found an impossible task: moving as fast as they were, it would be neither prudent nor safe to remain behind to look for a signal flag; and, even if it were, the country through which they were riding was too flat and wooded to offer a point of altitude for observation. So he galloped on with the others, forced to ignore his orders.

As the column neared Beaver Dam, the skies grew dark and rain and snow began falling. Into the village galloped the horsemen, so suddenly and so unexpectedly that they were able to capture the telegraph operator before he could tap out a message on the only key they had encountered that was still in touch with Richmond. They then entered upon a campaign of complete destruction. Twenty wooden buildings, including a large new freight house, the telegraph office, passenger depot, engine house, water tank, and several outhouses, as well as hundreds of cords of wood stacked alongside the track, were set afire. A sheet of flame shot high above the

surrounding woods, illuminating the countryside for miles.
Wrote one of the participants: "The dark forms of our soldiers jumping and dancing around it seemed from a distance
like demons on some hellish sport." [27]

While the flames still licked angrily into the sky, a train
was heard approaching from Richmond. It rolled into sight
and stopped; about twenty-five men got down from its cars
and fired a harmless volley. When the advance guard of Kilpatrick's party charged them, they fled into the woods and
the train backed hurriedly away.

Shortly afterward, as the raiders turned their backs on the
flaming mass, rain began falling furiously. Sharp winds
whipped it into sleet and drove it along with such stinging
force that men rode with their eyes closed and heads bowed.
When nightfall set in it was so dark trees along the roadside
were obliterated. "So complete darkness I never saw," wrote
one of the riders. "Men depended entirely on the instinct of
their horses, and the whole command on a Negro to guide
them." [28]

Bushwhackers annoyed the column continually, their shots
coming from both sides of the road. In a number of places
barricades had been made of fence rails and trees, and from
behind these barriers there was brief firing as the raiders approached. Flashes in the darkness ahead invariably indicated
an obstruction of some sort.

From a barricade at one point the firing was more stubborn
than usual, and a dozen or so of the raiders were deployed on
each flank to come in from behind. There were minutes of
waiting while the Unionists crawled through the darkness,
and then Pennsylvania and Indiana voices yelled from the rear
for a surrender. Twelve Confederates, two of them lieutenants, complied.

The alarm had by now been spread generally among the
Southerners. Lee wired Richmond that enemy cavalry was
moving on the left and right flanks, one column in the

direction of Charlottesville, another toward Frederick's Hall. His message was sent from Orange Court House, and with it went an appeal that Bradley Johnson be notified.[29]

Johnson already was in the saddle. Most of his Maryland Line was on picket duty along the Pamunkey as far as New Kent Court House, leaving him only seventy-five men in camp, but with sixty of them and two pieces of artillery he was on his way to locate the raiders.[30]

However, back along the Rapidan there was as yet no indication the raid had been discovered. Signal Officer John Wiggins, looking down from Garnett's Mountain, reported as dusk set in: "No change in the enemy's position in our front. The enemy seem to be ignorant of the move as they are all very quiet. Some of their regiments have been drilling today." [31]

Richmond on the other hand was now fully aware of the raid. The first news that came into the city was to the effect that a heavy column of Federals had appeared in the neighborhood of Frederick's Hall, and there was immediate consternation: it was well known that the reserve artillery of the Army of Northern Virginia was quartered there, and without adequate protection. It was even reported that the artillery had been captured, but later it was learned that the raiders had avoided that point and crossed the railroad to the east. Passengers arriving on the R. F. & P. train from Fredericksburg said that the Yankee force consisted of one brigade of cavalry and several pieces of artillery. Word also was received, before Dahlgren's men succeeded in cutting the telegraph wires at Frederick's Hall, that Custer had been repulsed near Charlottesville and had retired.

Richmond also was getting reports of the advancing column. Dr. L. B. Anderson, captain of the North Anna Home Guards, had been several miles away from his home at Hewlett's Station visiting a patient when he got word the Federals were at Beaver Dam. He hurried back, collecting his men along the way. Moving carefully through woods and fields, he chose a path that avoided all roads; and when Gloskoski sent up rockets, the doctor and his band were observing from a point only a few yards away.

Back along the Rapidan, General Meade sat down to prepare a letter to his wife. It was optimistic in tone, written without knowledge of the hardships facing the horsemen: ". . . My cavalry expedition for Richmond got off last night, and at two A.M., the last I heard from them, they were getting on famously, not having met anyone or being, as far as they could tell, discovered by the enemy. I trust they will be successful; it will be the greatest feat of the war, if they do succeed, and will immortalize them all. Young Dahlgren, with his one leg, went along with them. The weather begins to look suspicious, and tonight we have a little rain . . ." [32]

Toward Richmond, where Kilpatrick's horsemen were moving, the "little rain" continued as a storm of sleet, hail, rain, and snow, and travel became more and more laborious. But on and on without halt went the raiders. In time they forded Little River and, a short while later, made their way across New Found River, both tributaries of the North and South Annas, principal sources of the Pamunkey. As they cleared each stream, Kilpatrick breathed with some relief: he knew that in a few hours, if the downpour failed to slacken, these gentle rivulets would turn into churning torrents and push wildly out of their banks.

At nine o'clock, with animals and men tired and soggy, the order was given to halt for an hour or two of rest. As of the moment, prospects seemed bright. The South Anna was the only stream still ahead, and that could be crossed via Ground Squirrel Bridge. Kilpatrick, crawling from his horse, seemed smaller in stature. His blue overcoat crackled under its covering of ice, and the soggy brim of his hat sagged over his beaklike nose, making him look like some bloodthirsty hawk in search of prey.

As the hungry soldiers tried hurriedly to make coffee and cook enough food to ease their hunger, the Confederate patriot, Dr. Anderson, North Anna Home Guard captain, continued to watch them from cover. Some of his men wanted to shoot into the mass of blue-coated invaders, but the doctor made them desist. It was his conviction that this entire column was moving into a trap, which he intended to help close. As soon as the Federals climbed back into their saddles, he went to a nearby home and wrote a dispatch to be forwarded to Richmond as quickly as possible.[33]

On a parallel road to the west of Kilpatrick's path, Dahlgren was approaching the South Anna, finding travel steadily more difficult in the rain and intense darkness. At ten o'clock he forded the stream and pressed on. It was almost impossible to keep the column closed up, a circumstance that took its toll in the wilderness of Virginia's winding roads. About fifty of the men became lost somewhere in the confusion at the rear, wandering around on their own until they rejoined their companions at dawn. If the young colonel was aware of their absence, he gave no indication. His mind was focused on progress, for he had many more miles to cover than Kilpatrick, and they must be covered on schedule if the attack on Richmond was to be simultaneous. The determined spirit he was displaying encouraged his men. One of his troopers later observed for the records: "Who would complain of weariness when he looked at the colonel, still weak from his wound, riding along quietly, uncomplainingly, ever vigilantly watching every incident of the march?"[34]

On through the black night rode the columns, each following its individual route. Tired, hungry, sleepy, they trudged along, scattering copies of Abe Lincoln's amnesty proclamation and wondering what the morrow would bring.

They were not the only soldiers braving the night. Over the mountains beyond Charlottesville more Rebels were organizing to take to the trail of the raiders. Young Brigadier

General Thomas L. Rosser, informed of the movement on Richmond, had hastily called out his cavalry, and now he led them through the freezing rain, on a ride that would take them over Afton Mountain, a hazardous journey after dark even in fair weather.[35] For days they would ride, surviving on mule meat a part of the time; and after one of the roughest weeks in their lives they would be back in camp without even laying eyes on the Federal raiders.

North of the Potomac, newspapers were coyly trying to print the news and still not give away army secrets. Not many hours after Kilpatrick's horsemen crossed the Rapidan, New Yorkers were reading a news item in the *Herald* that might have been disastrous in a day of faster communication and more alert intelligence. It was the handiwork of an enterprising reporter stationed at the headquarters of the Army of the Potomac along the Rapidan. So far in advance was it written that it missed the exact hour of the raid's start by one full day.[36] It also confused the route taken by the column and its activities immediately after leaving camp. But the remainder of the report was remarkably correct. The only censorship the journalist imposed upon himself concerned the exact object of the raid, which he termed "a grand expedition." He told that the march was toward the junction of the Virginia Central and R. F. & P., and that Dahlgren was to swing wide by way of Frederick's Hall to destroy the artillery, railroad, and telegraph lines; but nowhere in the article was there mention of the Confederate capital. That this city, the most important goal of the Union army, lay in the general direction of the raid was left for the reader to surmise.

In Richmond the editor of the *Daily Dispatch* was printing all the news available to him, and, for a journalist shut up in a beleaguered city, he was doing a commendable job of reporting. Preparing his account for the Tuesday morning edition, he correctly denied the rumors that General Lee and the Second Corps artillery had been captured. And at one point in his account he wrote prayerfully: "The raid is no doubt intended to interrupt communications between General Lee's army and Richmond, but it is hoped that, like Stoneman's raid last spring, it may prove a failure."

7

The Attack

DAYLIGHT CAME, and with it weather that was cloudy, cold, rainy, and threatening snow. It found both columns in motion, each having suffered through a night notable for its horrors of sleet and ice. Dahlgren had ridden until 2:00 A.M.; then, realizing he was losing men in the darkness, he had called a rest nine miles from Goochland Court House. At a small grocery store that stood near the roadside he halted, drenched with rain, and was helped from his horse. Someone asked if he was tired, and he replied with spirit, "We'll have some supper and two hours' sleep, then you'll see how bright I am." [1]

Kilpatrick's troopers, after stopping briefly before midnight, had kept constantly to the saddle, and for them there was activity a-plenty. Ground Squirrel Bridge was never reached. A Negro employed as guide led them on a route—through ignorance, Kilpatrick believed—that veered farther toward Ashland, and there the column encountered enemy pickets. Several were captured, and from them it was learned that 2000 Confederate infantry and six pieces of artillery were stationed at a railroad bridge only a short distance from town.

Announcement of this strength, greatly exaggerated, caused Kilpatrick to lose some of the sparkle and dash with which he had advanced up to this point. Such a force could mean trouble, and he was so upset by the threat of it that he divided his column. Major Hall of the Sixth New York Cavalry, who had been entangled in the confusion associated with assembling the various units at Stevensburg prior to the start of the raid, was instructed to lead 450 men in a determined attack on the bridge, more to cover the movements of the main column than to inflict damage. Thus, while Hall moved in one direction, the remainder of the raiders headed for the South Anna, crossing just at daylight three miles above Ashland. As they rode, behind them in the distance could be heard the disturbance stirred up by their comrades-in-arms, giving Kilpatrick confidence that the enemy was deceived and unaware of his approach. With eagerness he pushed forward, slowing up once, below Ashland, long enough to destroy a section of the R. F. & P. track.

By 10:00 A.M., March 1, Kilpatrick was at a point on Brook Turnpike five miles from Richmond.[2] In the distance Rebel artillery still blasted away at Hall—guarantee enough to Kilpatrick that the Richmond defenders were sending all their available reserves in the direction of the firing. Any group would react in such a manner, he concluded, and developments closer at hand made the opinion seem sound. Both white and colored people who came along the road out of Richmond reported that as far as they knew no attack on the city was anticipated, that only a small force occupied the works along the turnpike ahead. Someone had a copy of a local newspaper just off the press. Its news was calm, giving no warning of trouble other than an unconfirmed report that a brigade of Yankee cavalry had crossed the Rapidan.

But Kilpatrick moved cautiously. If he had reasoned back at Stevensburg that Richmond was a place that could be stormed easily, he apparently failed to think so now. Gone was any idea of bursting into the city. Although he could not be sure, somehow he had faith that Butler would be attacking from the east at Bottom's Bridge, as called for in original plans.

Thus bothered by uncertainties, Kilpatrick gave his orders. Skirmishers spread out toward the city. The drive and thrust that had marked the column on its way past Spotsylvania and Beaver Dam and Ashland had disappeared. Why? Maybe "Kilcavalry" was delaying until he heard Butler's guns, or those of Dahlgren to the south. Maybe he was concerned over those 2000 infantrymen that Hall was supposed to be facing somewhere to his rear. Maybe it was stage fright, or maybe it was the danger implied by a local rustic on horseback who appeared from somewhere and went galloping madly cross-country in the direction of the city.

In any case, Kilpatrick suddenly adopted caution, even before the enemy in force was sighted. Scattered Rebels appeared at a bridge across a stream and hurriedly retreated, but not before several were captured. Others who had been hiding in the woods, frightened now by the size of the advancing column, came out and surrendered.

Soon more pickets were encountered. The advance guard drove them back and then went on to overrun a small infantry force in rifle pits beyond. Farther along appeared the first line of works, thrown up to guard a bridge. Skirmishers found it unmanned.

Slowly the column moved forward, with men listening and looking all the while for some evidence that Dahlgren had made his way into the city from the other side and was ready now to cooperate in the attack or to ride out again with mission accomplished. For nearly two miles the advance continued unopposed, and when resistance did finally come it was in the form of both artillery and rifle fire, from behind earthworks stretching to the right and left of the turnpike. Kilpatrick noted the time: 1:00 P.M.

Minutes passed, and the firing behind the earthworks grew hotter. It was carried on largely by riflemen, but as the Federals deployed in the face of this growing stubbornness, the Rebels put additional heavy guns to use.

Kilpatrick was puzzled: Richmond was supposed to be unprotected by regular troops. But the men manning these guns were not acting like amateurs.

Along the entire line guns blazed, the pace at times stepping up almost to the crescendo of a drawn battle. The day wore on. If Dahlgren were attacking on the other side of the city, there was little chance of hearing the noise he was making.

Up ahead, leading Kilpatrick's advance, was an officer of the regular army, Brigadier General H. E. Davies, Jr., a capable soldier. To his trained eye the enemy's position seemed a good one. For a thousand yards in front of the works the country was open and perfectly level, affording no cover and no position where the Union artillery could be used to advantage. On the other hand, the big guns that the Rebels were firing commanded the approach along the road and had perfect range of the entire ground, while an enfilade could be hurled in upon the invaders by two pieces on the right and four on the left, all of which were being heard from with regularity. To make matters worse for the invaders, the surrounding fields were so soft and muddy that it would be impossible for cavalry to maneuver over them except as skirmishers.

Having sized up the situation, Davies ordered the Fifth New York to deploy on foot and move as far as practicable toward the earthworks. Then he directed the remainder of his command to form while he went forward to examine the ground. Advancing cautiously, he concluded that the best method of attack would be to send forward a strong party of dismounted men on the left, under cover of some houses, and, when they became well engaged, to make the main attack down the road, covered by artillery. Accordingly, 500 troopers were taken from the different regiments and sent off afoot, armed with carbines, under instructions to make as much of a diversion as possible.

Davies waited. Soon his ear told him the 500 men had come within range, for Rebel musketry fire increased with a deafening rattle along the point toward which they moved. He rode forward to direct the main charge, but just then an order arrived instructing him to fall back and take the road to Meadow Bridge, covering the rear of the division, on the Mechanicsville pike.[3]

Kilpatrick's decision for a withdrawal—critics would say it showed his tendency to turn and run at the wrong time—had come at a moment when his lieutenants were extending and strengthening their lines in preparation for a general advance. It was influenced by an idea the enemy was rapidly receiving support, both of infantry and artillery. And this belief was strengthened by the manner in which the Confederates stepped up their firing at sight of Davies' 500 in their front. A convincing effect. The attack that had seemed so simple on paper, so foolproof when outlined to Lincoln and Stanton, now took on an air of impossibility. Certainly it was too great a task for just 3000 troopers, and that was all he had left since detaching the 450 under Hall. And by this time, too, he was confident that Dahlgren had failed to cross the river and storm into the city from the south.

The scene before Kilpatrick was far from cheery—growing darkness, leaden skies, smoke and fog, mud and muck, spitting rain, obviously on the verge of turning to snow, and lurking behind the earthworks a foe who had not given one hint that he was thinking about retreat or surrender. Moreover, Butler had never been heard from, and there was no evidence he would be. In this situation the cavalry leader made up his mind that "an attempt to enter the city at that point would but end in a bloody failure." [4]

He gave his orders, and gradually the firing in front of the earthworks died away in the darkness. The column turned about slowly as soldiers who had been on foot found their horses and swung into the saddle. On to the north, across the Chickahominy at Meadow Bridge, they moved, tired, wet, hungry, and sleepy, to huddle in a camp near Mechanicsville. Dozens of men—Kilpatrick put it at sixty—were left behind, either dead or wounded. The Rebels were estimated to have lost 200.[5]

Along the way Davies and seven fellow officers drew up at an oyster saloon on the side of the road and ordered supper. The proprietor set before them eggs, bacon, honey, and bread —and then the bill: $85.40 in Confederate currency. It was settled for $32 Confederate and $2.00 Union.[6]

Throughout the advance toward Richmond, Joe Gloskoski had been wasting his time trying to pick up Dahlgren's signals. Nothing but frustration greeted his efforts, and this was puzzling because he knew that Lieutenant Reuben Bartley, an experienced signal officer sent from headquarters, was riding with the other column and also should be trying to establish contact. Working against Gloskoski were the woods, mist, smoke, and his lack of knowledge of the companion detail's whereabouts. But he was not unduly worried. He reasoned that the sound of the firing along Brook Turnpike would certainly be warning enough to Dahlgren that Richmond was not to be taken by surprise.

As Kilpatrick's troops moved back and the gunfire fell away to silence, more than one ear was trained to pick up sounds from the south side of the city. If the other column had made its way in from that direction, there was no evidence of it. Everything was still and silent and taunting. No signal, visible or oral, came to inform them of the smaller detachment's progress. It was not known to them that Bradley Johnson's Maryland Line, edging up on the flank at Yellow Tavern during the morning, had grabbed off an officer and five men bearing Dahlgren's message intended to inform Kilpatrick that he would attack at dusk.[7]

Moving back, Kilpatrick gradually began to distrust his own judgment. Scouts and spies told him on the way to Meadow Bridge that during the day the entire available force of the enemy had been concentrated where the attacks had been made, and that there were no troops on the road from Mechanicsville to the city. Had he been wrong to withdraw?

Soon after crossing Meadow Bridge, the raiders swung into camp and dropped with fatigue from their horses. They made a miserable picture, cold, wet, muddy, with rain, sleet, and snow beating down upon them and not a single tent for shelter. "It was a wild Walpurgis night," recorded one of them, "such a night as Goethe paints in his Faust while demons hold revel in the forests of the Brocken." [8] One of their first acts was to attempt to start fires.[9] In most instances it was a forlorn effort, but a few were successful, and onto the spits went poultry and other items gathered up along the route from Stevensburg. Hovering in the outskirts of their camp were the contrabands, an increasing following of Negroes who had attached themselves to the column under the belief that it was a sure way to freedom.

Kilpatrick was not prepared to settle down for the night. Still in his mind was the suspicion that he had made a mistake to withdraw. It grew larger, and by ten o'clock he was determined to try once more to enter the city. Accordingly, he ordered two separate detachments of 500 men each to move in on the Mechanicsville road while he remained behind with the artillery and other troops to protect their rear at Meadow Bridge. The second-guessers would call this his third mistake. They saw as his first the division of the column back at Stevensburg, and the second, his failure to storm into Richmond.[10] But wise or unwise, this third error was not for execution. Before the two forces could be started, Confederates advancing from the direction of Hanover Court House made contact and drove in his pickets.

Kilpatrick sent word for a strong line to be thrown out to push the enemy back, but this was no easy task, for it was soon learned that the attackers were Wade Hampton's regular cavalry. The Rebel leader, having so few troops at his command, had waited until night to strike. By this time the snow had become mixed with rain, and out in the inky darkness the gunfire of the Southerners, including thunderous blasts from two pieces of artillery that Hampton carried with him, sparked like fireflies on a summer night. Union horses were panicked by the noise of shells crashing through the trees. The fourteenth of these cannon blasts was the signal for the Rebels on foot to charge.[11]

The Southerners came rushing out of the darkness, taking advantage of the reflection from the campfires, and it was an advantage that told. The attack was orderly, the defense scattered and confused.

Many of the Union soldiers, after more than forty-eight hours in the saddle, were so exhausted that they acted as if in a nightmare. An orderly shook a snoozing officer and pointed to his saddled horse. The officer got up, buckled on his sword, and started to mount. When he put his foot in the stirrup, the saddle slipped off and fell to the ground. Realizing that the orderly had neglected to fasten the girths properly, the officer sleepily put the saddle on again and tightened it to his satisfaction. Then he mounted and kicked with his spurs, only to find that the horse had never been untied from a tree.[12]

The affair, confusion and all, lasted only a short time. In the face of the determined attack, the Federals soon sidled off to the east toward Old Church, groping their way along a road they had not intended to follow.[13] Some, unable to locate their horses in the dark, were on foot, plodding through mud over their shoetops. Others had left in such a panic they had not taken time to bother with saddles, and for the remainder of the raid they would be riding bareback. But the immediate problem was to get away from the angry guns of Hampton's cavalry. Mile after mile along the sloppy road they struggled, tired, sleepy, and downhearted; and if only out of great personal relief they were high in their praise of Kilpatrick when he called a halt before dawn.[14]

But even then there was no rest for the invaders. In the snowy, rainy darkness it was impossible to find places fit for repose, and the Rebels continued to heckle them with pot shots. But daylight brought a pleasant surprise to some of the weary and hungry Union troopers. Moving bundles of fodder in a nearby barnyard, they uncovered a cache of sweet potatoes and immediately got a first-class roasting under way.

During the closing hours of Tuesday, while Kilpatrick was trying to fend off Hampton's angry horsemen, General Meade, back at Brandy Station, must have suspected that all was not well with the raid. Before going to his couch that stormy night, he dispatched a report to General Halleck at Washington. It began with uncertain news—"no intelligence has been received from Kilpatrick's command since yesterday at two A.M."—and wound up with announcement that Custer was back after a damaging blow at Charlottesville. Custer had found the railroad bridge over the Rivanna River too strongly guarded to risk attack, but he had destroyed a highway bridge, captured an enemy camp, a Virginia militia flag, 500 horses, two wagons filled with bacon, and six caissons loaded with ammunition, and, as a final stroke, had burned three large flour mills.[15]

But Kilpatrick and his men had no time for thought of what had happened or was happening at either Stevensburg or Charlottesville. At dawn on Wednesday they heard anew from the Rebels. Peppery firing sounded in the growing daylight, and Union pickets were forced back upon the column. Kilpatrick endured this annoyance until 8:00 A.M. Then he ordered his men back into the saddle—all of those who had saddles and all of those afoot for whom horses could be obtained—and on they trudged to Old Church, there to take a stand and drive off the last charge of the enemy.[16]

After the pestering from the Rebels had ended, Kilpatrick stayed on, hoping for some word from Dahlgren. This would seem the most likely path for the other column to follow. And, anyway, there certainly should be no trouble in picking up the trail he and his men were leaving as they struggled to reach Butler's lines.

The hours of the afternoon slipped by with no change. As night approached, Kilpatrick moved out again, this time in the direction of New Kent Court House, where he knew he would come in contact with Butler's lines. But the march continued no farther than Tunstall's Station. Near that point 300 of Dahlgren's men, coaxing their horses along the muddy roads, splashed up in the rear, bringing the first news from the missing column. What they had to tell was not good. Their leader, Captain John F. B. Mitchell of the Second New York Cavalry, reported that Dahlgren and about a hundred men had become separated from the remainder of the column and had not been heard from since.

Mitchell gave other details that added to Kilpatrick's woes. After the rest near Goochland, he said, Dahlgren rode on, stopping at the home of the Horton family, in sight of the James River and just twenty-one miles from Richmond. There he ordered Mitchell, with the Second New York Cavalry detachment of 100 men, to proceed down the Kanawha Canal skirting the river on the north. As he moved, taking with him the ambulance, prisoners, and led horses, he was to destroy generally, burning such things as canal locks, canal boats, mills, and all the grain he could find. When he arrived at Westham Creek, about six miles from the Rebel capital, he was to send the ambulances and prisoners to Hungary Station, where they would meet the main column under Kilpatrick, and then he was to dash directly toward the city. Dahlgren in the meantime would cross the James River at a point to be shown him by Martin Robinson, and come into Richmond from the south. If they failed to meet there, Mitchell was to push on and overtake Kilpatrick.

It all sounded easy, and Dahlgren was filled with enthusiasm. He called for the torpedoes, turpentine, and oakum, and passed a supply of each to Mitchell. Then he sloshed off with his detail, some 400 men, all armed and ready to carry out their leader's orders. It was evident from the start that no pleasure would come of this jaunt. As they galloped away, the mud underfoot spattered against the horses' bellies and even up into the faces of the riders.

Mitchell watched them disappear before moving off with his slower caravan of vehicles and horses. As he advanced, a part of his men—those who escorted the ambulances—took the river road, while the others followed the canal towpath. Their progress was slow, for they concentrated on pillage and destruction. At farmhouses they took what they wanted, hacked up furniture, and applied the firebrand generally. Horses and cattle they could not take along were shot in the field.

The job got bigger. Along the way six busy grist mills filled with grain and flour, one of them the prosperous and historic Dover Mills, were set afire.[17] Also burned were a canal lock and the coal mine at Manakin's Ferry.

At one point they drew up, gloating. Before them were some of the finest estates in Virginia. The New York *Times* correspondent covering the raid said that they were peopled by some of the most aristocratic residents of the state, by "families who boasted of their long line of ancestors, the number of their Negroes, their broad acres—in fact, where the feudal lords reigned supreme both over the white trash and the Negro in bondage." [18]

There was "Sabot Hill," the charming home of James A. Seddon, Confederate Secretary of War, lawyer, ex-congressman, member of the peace convention held in Washington in

'61. He was a man of great refinement, wealth, and experience in public affairs, and his wife was the beautiful Sallie Bruce, descended from a large and prominent southern Virginia family. Her sister, Ellen, also a belle and the wife of James M. Morson, another aristocrat, was next door at "Dover" plantation. Close by, too, was "Eastwood," residence of Plumer Hobson, married to a daughter of former Governor Henry A. Wise. Refinement and hospitality, accompanied by the ease of plenty, were to be found at these fine homesteads, all set down in a sort of circle of society, with everything about them of the very best. One servant on duty there, distinguished for his courtly manner at social gatherings, had cost his master $2500.[19]

Mitchell's men wasted no time on ceremony. Three times the Morson home was set afire and as often extinguished by house servants. The family cellar was pried open and from it taken wine of ancient vintage, later quaffed from silver goblets as the drinkers rode along on horseback.[20]

At the Seddon estate they put the torch to a well-filled barn, the corn houses, and stables. Then they galloped away without paying any attention to the big house. There they would have crossed paths with Ulric Dahlgren.

The young colonel, on sighting the Seddon estate, had shown no interest in barns and outbuildings, but had ridden directly to the mansion. Struggling down from his saddle and leaning heavily on his crutch, he stalked with wooden leg up the steps to the door and knocked loudly. A servant swung the portal back upon Sallie Bruce, her beauty still evident despite the plumpness of middle age. There was about her a haughty, dignified air.

"I'm Colonel Dahlgren," the intruder said.

He got no further, for the woman's manner changed. "Are you related to Admiral Dahlgren?" she asked.

"I'm his son, Ulric."

The woman smiled prettily. "Then I knew you as a boy,

and I knew your father when I was one of your mother's schoolmates in Philadelphia. He was a beau of mine."

For a moment the war was forgotten. The young colonel doffed his campaign hat and, bowing awkwardly, swung it in a wide sweep.

"Come in," invited Mrs. Seddon, leading the way into the parlor.

"Uncle Charles," she said to the servant who had opened the door, "go down and bring up some of the blackberry wine of our 1844 vintage."

Soon the lady and the young colonel were toasting each other over silver goblets. As they laughed and chatted, the woman's thoughts flashed back and she relived her youth through the inspiration of this young raider who now had suddenly lost his fierceness. But finally duty called, and the soldier stumped back to his horse, this time with a graceful farewell and repeated assurance that no harm should come to the mansion.

Over at "Eastwood" the story was different. There sat Plumer Hobson and his father-in-law, the former governor, who had come the night before for a visit. Into their presence suddenly rushed servants with exciting reports: Yankees were in the neighborhood, and smoke was rising above the trees. The news was the forerunner of a typical Rebel exit. The two men rushed out to the barns and galloped away on horses already saddled and waiting. As the fleeing pair approached the nearest patch of woods, Sergeant D. H. Schofield of the Fifth New York Cavalry rode up to the home with a detail of soldiers and surrounded it.

Mitchell's path of destruction now reached as far as Manakin's Ferry. At that point he learned there would be nothing more to destroy until he got within three miles of Richmond, so he concentrated his men on the river road. Just before combining his column, he came upon the tracks of Dahlgren's party, a surprising development, for he assumed the colonel had crossed the river and was galloping toward the Rebel capital. Up ahead at Jude's Ferry, two miles from Dover Mills, another surprise awaited him. Swinging by the neck from a tree beside the road was the body of Martin Robinson, the guide.

It was not until midafternoon that Mitchell learned what had happened to the Negro. At three-thirty he came upon Dahlgren's men resting at Short Pump, about eight miles from Richmond. Martin, he was told, had misled the column, taking it to a point on the river where there was no sign of a ford, and where the water, swollen by rains, was too deep and treacherous to attempt a crossing. The young colonel, suspecting treachery, had ripped off a strap from his bridle and ordered an immediate hanging.[21] No patience, this; no thought that ignorance might have played a hand. Confederate Secretary of War Seddon would say of the execution that the Federal officer "sought to cover the timidity that shrank from trying a doubtful ford by an act of savage vengeance on his Negro guide, who indeed merited his fate, but not at the hands of the enemy." [22]

As soon as Mitchell arrived, Dahlgren made plans for the final ride into Richmond. Before leaving Short Pump, corn confiscated along the way was scattered for the horses. When this had been eaten, ambulances, prisoners, and the led animals were sent off in the direction of the firing, now plainly audible and confidently recognized as Kilpatrick's attack on the city. It was the last the raiders would see of them.

While the column rested, three Rebels in militia uniform came galloping up in the rain on splendid mounts and were flagged down without a shot. Then, for security reasons, they were subjected to a bit of questioning. Why the hurry and where were they going? No hurry—they just belonged to the Richmond City Battalion, led by General Lee's son, Custis. And they were on their way to stand picket against the very Yankees who had bagged them.

At five o'clock Dahlgren resumed his march toward Richmond. He followed the old Three-Chop Road, a thoroughfare famed in Revolutionary days. It led onto the Westham Plank Road at Westham.[23]

At a point five miles from the city, bullets began to whine out of the fast-growing dusk. They poured into the Fifth Michigan, riding in advance. The Michiganders wavered, fell back momentarily, and then, forming again, pushed ahead.

But the volleys continued to come in cracking echoes from the trees. Finally, as darkness came on, the Federals determined that they were being fired on by dismounted skirmishers. The only way to proceed, as they saw it, was to charge over the enemy lines. This they did for two and a half miles, capturing 200 prisoners and losing heavily in killed and wounded. All at once the Rebel fire picked up in volume. It blazed with such fury that Dahlgren was convinced reinforcements had arrived from within the city; and this conviction made his attack seem hopeless. Whirling about, he gave the order to retire.[24]

As they fell back, Mitchell was directed to take command of the rear guard and keep as much closed up as possible.[25] But in the intense darkness the withdrawal became a confused wrangle. To make matters worse, rain and snow pelted the men in their faces, combining with the impenetrable night to obliterate the path of retreat. After some time the riders bringing up the rear noticed that the column ahead had halted. A lieutenant was sent forward to investigate. He brought back disturbing news: Colonel Dahlgren and scores of others had pushed on and, in the darkness, had broken contact with the remainder of the column. Mitchell was suddenly confronted with unexpected responsibility. He sent scouts in all directions to search and shout and listen, but their efforts were futile. Only stillness and occasionally angry shots from the Rebels back on the Westham road greeted their ears.

Mitchell realized he must now depend upon his own re-

sources. On along the road toward Hungary Station he struggled, fumbling and guessing in the dark. At one point the
advance guard met enemy pickets and drove them back.
Ahead could be seen campfires—at the Station, it was assumed.
The rattle of small arms, interspersed with the occasional
boom of a cannon, sounded louder, ever more threatening.
Officers came together for a council. What should they do—
turn back or make a dash for it? All were in accord: dash for
it. So riders bunched together and galloped forward, shouting
and cheering loudly to give an air of belligerence. But the
Rebels didn't scare. Instead, they sent a galling fire out of the
darkness, from the bushes and a loghouse near the road, and
the Federals fell back.

Mitchell now turned about and sent his men along roads
in various directions, each group advancing until checked by
enemy skirmishers. This uncertain and desperate flight was
continued, except for a brief rest in the predawn cold, until
finally they came up with Kilpatrick near Tunstall's Station.
Dozens of men had been lost during the ride, either felled by
enemy bullet or entangled and lost in the thick growth of
trees. Mitchell could count but 260 in the column with which
he had escaped.

It was now obvious to Kilpatrick that the raid had failed
utterly. This daring undertaking, on which he at one time
would have staked his life, suddenly seemed completely foolish. Many factors had combined to upset it, all pointing to the
fact that Kilpatrick, as well as his superiors, had acted without
complete knowledge of the situation. Richmond's defenses
were stronger than anticipated, or so it seemed.[26] The raiders
under his command had been able to get nowhere near Belle
Isle or Libby Prison, and, as far as he knew, neither had those
with Dahlgren.

Under the circumstances, as sad as they were, the only
course left Kilpatrick was to strike toward Butler's lines before the Confederates rounded up their forces and wiped him

out completely. And he would have to follow a route he had not planned to take. As outlined back at headquarters, he was to go toward West Point. This was now impossible, for Hampton had forced him onto a different road, and his face at the moment was turned toward Williamsburg.

While Kilpatrick rode east, Richmond waited tensely, not knowing what to expect. The last twenty-four hours had seemed endless. When news of the raid had reached the War Department during the night of the 29th, Colonel Walter H. Stevens, commanding the capital's defenses, issued orders for artillery to be moved to three strategic points and for guards at road intersections to the north to be doubled. Daylight found these dispositions in order.

Tuesday morning, just before the Federals showed up on the edge of the city, Stevens rode out to examine the defense layout, and was pleased with what he saw. In the distance toward Ashland he could hear artillery barking away busily, and he wondered about its exact meaning. But his chief worry was closer at hand—Richmond. He swung his horse about and returned to headquarters, barely getting settled behind his desk before a dispatch arrived announcing that the raiders were in front of the Rebel pickets along Brook Turnpike. Without delay he mounted again and hurried toward the northern outskirts.

Inside the city, excitement grew rapidly as couriers and horsemen from the country brought news that the enemy was within the outer fortifications—a column of 5000 cavalry, they said.[27] Then came the Honorable James Lyons, one of the city's most distinguished citizens, to report that the Federals were shelling his house, only a mile and a half away.

Out on Brook Turnpike, Stevens was preparing to throw all his force—about 500 men and six pieces of artillery—into the face of the advancing foe. Now the only troops remaining in the city to stem an attack from any other direction was the local defense brigade, an organization set up by act of Confederate Congress as a result of Stoneman's raid and others earlier in the war. This brigade differed from the state militia in that its members were enlisted for the duration of the conflict, were uniformed and equipped by the government, and were controlled by the War Department.[28] It was comprised of five battalions, one each from the Armory, Arsenal, Tredegar Iron Works, Navy, and government departments—the last of these organized into the City Battalion. All in all, its membership was a motley group--clerks and artisans, men too old and boys too young to join the army, and some soldiers assigned to the shops in Richmond because of certain skills they possessed. Early in the war the machinery from the United States Arsenal at Harpers Ferry had been commandeered by the South and moved to Richmond. There it had been set up in what was known as the Virginia Armory, at the foot of Fifth Street, between the canal and the river. Three companies of the battalion came from this busy plant. A fourth volunteered from a carbine factory on Seventh Street, and another was formed at a nearby harness shop. They were ready and willing, and they had been receiving special training under Custis Lee, tapped for the duty by none other than President Jefferson Davis.

As the morning advanced and Kilpatrick's force out on Brook Turnpike grew larger, crowds filled the streets and hovered around public buildings to learn what was happening. Mounted officers and couriers dashed wildly about. There was talk of evacuating government officials by railroad toward Danville.

In the early afternoon, above the rumble of guns in the northern outskirts, sounded the old bell on Capitol Square, the tocsin used to summon men to the defense of the city. At the Armory the starter took hold of the hand wheel and ran down the gates to the turbine water wheels.

This was an emergency!

Hundreds of machines—noisy trip hammers and smooth-running rollers turning out red-hot rifle barrels—came to a standstill. Through the departments hurried messengers, spreading the word: the enemy was in sight. Workers must hurry home, get into uniform, fill haversacks with cooked rations, and report back for duty. Out they rushed. On the street news awaited them: Yankee cavalry had ridden inside the main line of defense; one attack had been repulsed; others were expected.

A drizzling rain was falling as these men hurried away from their jobs to homes in various parts of the city—Sheep, Union, Church, Oregon and the other hills, seven in all. Many had risen at five o'clock, walked several miles, and been on their feet since reporting for work; now they would have to backtrack. It would be hours before they could cover the distance and get back into action.

Government clerks rushed away from Capitol Hill with their pockets bulging with inflated Confederate currency. It was payday, and they had just received their wages in five-dollar bills. One employee had time after receiving his money to buy a cord of wood for twenty dollars and a bushel of common white cornfield beans for sixty, and he had looked longingly at bacon, eight dollars a pound, but there he had balked. More of this meat was coming to town these days, someone had told him, and a decline in price could be expected.[29]

Off and on throughout the afternoon there were spurts of firing, informing the citizenry that the threat to Richmond was not lessening. Rain and sleet fell intermittently, thickening the atmosphere; and the thunder of artillery echoed with sodden, murky reverberations that seemed to shake every house. Caissons rolled in, were refilled with ammunition at the Armory, and hurried back to the scene of action. Everywhere there was alarm, and up at the White House of the Confederacy officials were noting that Jefferson Davis was in a terribly bad humor.[30]

Rumors ran wildly along the streets and were fed upon by old men, housewives, and children. Individual acts of bravery were acclaimed all out of proportion to their importance. One Joseph G. Dill, member of a local cavalry unit on picket duty a mile from Camp Lee, was given the status of a one-man army by the dignified Richmond *Inquirer:* he had finally been "surrounded, taken prisoner and carried off." The paper also announced next morning that "shells passed over the house of Thomas Johnston, whose family had a good view of the Yankees." Mr. Johnston saved his livestock by chasing it into the woods. It was said that the invaders had carried off Mrs. Patterson Allan, under indictment for treason in the Confederate District Court, but the *Dispatch* had its doubts: "This is only a rumor, and should be received with allowance."

By late afternoon enough boys from the Armory and the carbine factory—220—had returned to form their battalion. Away toward the west end of the city they hurried, all in rout step, for travel underfoot was miserable. Word had come in that an enemy force was following the course of the James River, and this band they hoped to head off. They had a lot of spirit and a lot of confidence. Their commander, Major Ford, an Englishman, was over six feet tall, straight as an arrow, and he was said to be an ex-cavalry officer. He rode up front on a fine chestnut stallion and led the way out Cary Street to the Westham Plank Road. As the column moved through the city, officers and soldiers of the regular army present on duty or passing through to commands caught stride and swung along, all privates for the occasion. Among these was the adjutant general of Beauregard's army. "No man with a heart could resist the anxious and appealing looks of the people," wrote a participant.[31] General Fitzhugh Lee was also in Richmond and might have gone along had he not departed earlier for the line of fortifications where Kilpatrick was attacking.[32]

Soon the home guardsmen met refugees fleeing in the path

of the invaders, driving before them herds of scrawny cattle.
There were wagons loaded with women and children and
furniture, and there were men riding horses drooping with
harness, taken along just to keep it from falling into the hands
of the Federals. It was rumored that the families of Secretary
Seddon and General Wise had been captured.

Near Westham the rout-steppers were overtaken by an ammunition wagon, and a halt was called for rounds to be distributed. It was then that the company of carbine-factory
boys, supplied before they left the city, forged ahead, impatient and excited. No one knew exactly where to expect the
enemy.

After drawing their supplies of ammunition, other companies of the battalion followed rapidly. When they got near
the point where the Westham road connected with the Three-
Chop Road, hot firing was heard ahead, and it was evident to
them that the carbine-factory company had become engaged.
Fumbling in the dark, some of them found a gap in a fence at
the side of the road and sloshed along through the mud to a
grove of young oaks. They knew they were in the vicinity
of the Benjamin W. Green home, "Roselawn," and soon they
came upon the carbine-factory boys, falling back with their
muzzle-loading rifles in the face of the faster-firing weapons
carried by the Federals. Guns blazed in the darkness. Suddenly someone cried, "Look out! They are flanking us!"
Major Ford, still astride his stallion, shouted, "Cease firing
and fall back!"

Back through the gap in the fence they came. Once again
in the road, the major tried to encourage a rally. In the darkness could be heard the galloping horses of the raiders and
now and then a cry of "Ride down the damn melish!" Young
Joe Haw, private in the Armory Battalion's Company A,
caught the spirit of the occasion: "Major Ford, still sitting on
his horse near the road facing the enemy, called on the men
to rally to him, and a few of us joined him there. After a

pause he remarked: 'We can do nothing here,' and began to retreat by the road. The Yankees were now right among the men in the field, and I could hear their oaths as they cried, 'Shoot the damned scoundrels!' Some of the men turned and fired right up in the faces of the enemy, showing pluck to the last." [33]

The retreat got little farther than the intersection of the Westham road, in the neighborhood of the Hicks farm, more sedately known as "Glenburnie." There the Armory Battalion encountered the battalion of government clerks, commanded by Captain John A. McAnerny, veteran of the Third Alabama recuperating from a severe battle wound. Farther back was more support, and galloping to the scene was Custis Lee.

But additional support was not needed. McAnerny handled his clerks like the veteran he was. Fifty men were sent ahead to fire one round and fall back. The others were told to lie flat on the ground and to await his signal. The one round sounded from the fifty men. A member of the group recorded: "It was pouring rain, cold and pitch dark. Still, we were near enough to hear their words of command. I fired my gun once." [34] Then they fell back, leading Dahlgren to believe it was the Armory Battalion making a final stand. [35] After this came the signal, and more guns went off in unison, booming like heavy artillery. Daylight would arrive before the total effect of that volley was known, but the immediate and obvious result was the end of the assault, for it was that blast which convinced Dahlgren that enemy reinforcements were at hand, and that further attack was useless. [36]

At their leader's command, the Federals turned back, leaving dead and wounded in their wake.

Now came the race for survival. Ahead lay only the black, sleety, snowy night. Pines and scrub trees grew thick and close along the roadside, and any rider so unfortunate as to touch one got an avalanche of water in his face. Often they had to stop to remove or make their way around fallen trees.

They traveled in single file, some of them sound asleep as they rode, and each time a turn was made, the word had to be passed down the line with care.

Back in Richmond an emergency still existed. Women and children kneeled at upstairs windows, some with ancient firearms, and waited and prayed. And down in the basement of Libby Prison, guards paced back and forth, casting wary glances at a six-foot-square mound of dirt thrown up that day in the center of the chamber. Beneath that shoveled heap lay the Confederate government's hasty answer to this new doorstep threat from the North—enough powder to blow the prison sky high.

But fate had combined with the timidity and bad planning of a cavalry leader who was to some men "a hell of a damned fool": the prison would not be blasted into bits.

8

A Boy Named Littlepage

Richmond awoke on March 2 to a light sprinkling of snow and a day bright and cool. Residents had fallen asleep the night before to the rumble of cannon and muskets in the distance. Mrs. Mary Boykin Chesnut, a housewife daily scribbling notes that were later to become well known as *A Diary from Dixie*, had gone to her couch after an absorbing session with *Romola* and after recording: "How hardened we grow to wars and war's alarms. The enemy's cannon—or our own—are thundering in my ears; and I was dreadfully afraid some infatuated and frightened friend would come in to cheer, to comfort, and to interrupt me. Am I the same poor soul who fell on her knees and prayed and wept and fainted, as the first guns boomed against Fort Sumter?" [1]

Off in fortifications encircling the city the faithful government clerks, mechanics, and laborers still fingered their weapons and stared expectantly along muddy approaches. But there was a cockiness about them now. They felt that 15,000 men might have stormed the Confederate stronghold in the beginning; yet this morning, hours later, twice that number would fail in the attempt. [2]

84

At daylight more dead and wounded were found and hauled into the city. It was a day of sadness.

Mourning for Richmonders centered mostly at the home of Captain Albert Ellery, chief clerk in the Second Auditor's Office—"dear old Captain Ellery." His body, shot through below the armpit, had been brought back by the local defense troops. They handled it tenderly, and what they said about it was in praise, for Ellery was a popular citizen and no ordinary patriot. At the war's beginning he had left a government job in Washington and come south to work for the Confederacy. Now, at sixty-three, he lay dead of a Dahlgren bullet. Reported the Richmond *Dispatch*: "He leaves an interesting wife and one child." [3] For him a spot in Hollywood Cemetery, a spot of honor close to other war heroes; and in his funeral cortege would move important people, the élite of Richmond. [4]

Also dead was Lieutenant John Sweeney of the Armory Battalion. The body, its lifeblood drained out during the night, had been found alongside the Westham Plank Road, pockets turned outward and rifled of a watch and $400, the salary he had received just before rushing off to the city's defense. A gold ring still circled one of his stiffened fingers; it had been saved by the darkness.

As the morning advanced, seventy-seven prisoners marched into the city, among them a lieutenant colonel, Allyne Litchfield; they had been rounded up during the night by Wade Hampton's cavalry. And soon there began to appear, quite to their friends' surprise, some of the men from the local defense units captured by Dahlgren's column. They gleefully told of their experience: so hard-pressed had become the raiders under Mitchell that before midnight they released most of the captives in desperation. [5]

Confederates sloshing through the mud out in the Mechanicsville neighborhood waited until daylight, then began gathering up the loot left by Kilpatrick in his hurried departure from his impromptu camp. Into the bag went a caisson full of ammunition, numbers of horses, a wagon and team, arms, rations, and clothing.

Rumors, fanned by the excitement of the moment, were reflected in morning newspaper reports. "Nothing is officially known of the whereabouts of General Kilpatrick," frankly admitted the Baltimore *Sun*. But the New York *Herald* reported that he had destroyed the Virginia Central Railroad from Beaver Dam to Hanover Junction and the R. F. & P. Railroad from Mattaponi Bridge to the Pamunkey River, a distance of forty miles. This paper also said that Kilpatrick had found the country through which he passed almost destitute of food for man or beast, making it necessary for him to push forward with all possible speed.

Back at Brandy Station, General Meade, dutifully writing his wife, said that, when last heard from, Kilpatrick was within thirty miles of Richmond. "Of course you can imagine our anxiety to know his fate," he added. "If he finds Richmond no better guarded than our information says it is, he will have a great chance of getting in and liberating all the prisoners, which is the great object of the movement. God grant he may, for their sakes and his." [6]

General Meade would not know until later how completely the raid was going to pieces. Kilpatrick had been driven onto the wrong road, off the route outlined originally back at headquarters, and Dahlgren was riding hard in an effort to find him. Never again would they meet. The young colonel was taking too wide a circuit, swinging to the northeast, via King William and King and Queen Counties, staging a desperate drive to reach Gloucester Point, on an entirely different neck of land from that along which the larger column was moving.

Early Wednesday morning Rebel scouts began to pick up Dahlgren's trail. He had crossed the Chickahominy during the early-morning hours, having in his column four commissioned officers, seventy-five privates, about fifty contrabands, and a number of led horses; and while waiting for his column to close up he had passed the time by chatting with the drivers of a Rebel ambulance train taking wounded to Richmond from the scene of Hampton's attack on Kilpatrick's camp. The teamsters, unaware of the identity of the horsemen gathered around them in the dark, boasted loudly that they had driven off the Yankees. In answer, Dahlgren announced: "You haven't driven us off. We're Yankees, and don't you think we're a nice lot of fellows?" But he got no satisfactory reply, either to that question or to questions he asked about roads in the neighborhood. So, rebuffed, he struck off in the black night, confident that sooner or later he would reach the Pamunkey.

It was eight o'clock in the morning when he rode out on the bank of that stream at Hanovertown. The river was high and the boat missing, but two brave lads, steeling themselves to the icy waters, swam across and located a skiff on the opposite side. Some time was consumed in crossing in this small craft, and then the column headed for Aylett's, on the Mattaponi.

While they rode, the countryside awakened to their presence.[7] Couriers on horseback headed for the courthouse to relay the news to a band of local men from the regular army on detached duty in King and Queen County. Represented were parts of several companies, and most of the members were sharpshooters. Arduous duty, chasing Union General Averell during December and early January, had earned them furloughs—with the understanding they would do picket duty while at home.

One outstanding unit was commonly known as Lee's Rangers, but more officially as Company H of the Ninth Virginia Cavalry. Its leader was Lieutenant James Pollard, a resourceful man.[8] When he heard that the raiders were trying to escape to Gloucester Point, he sent out couriers to spread the word and to watch roads and ferries. Then, without waiting further, he started in pursuit of Dahlgren with all the force left to him, a mere twenty-five.

Pollard's plan of action had been mapped out quickly. If the raiders were headed for Gloucester, they would have to cross the Mattaponi River, and the point at which they more than likely would attempt this crossing would be Dunkirk, where waited the only ferry left on the stream. But scouts soon informed Pollard that Dahlgren had found another way over the river. He had located a rowboat at Aylett's, farther down, and in this tiny craft had taken his men to the opposite bank, swimming the horses alongside.

The crossing had not been accomplished without a scene. From the cover of surrounding woods Rebel home guards blazed away at them angrily, causing general panic at the start. Dahlgren was furious to see his men run for cover. Riding out in front and daring the bullets of the bushwhackers, he let fly a stream of ridicule and abuse. "Return their fire!" he shouted, and in response enough resistance was built up to hold off the Confederates until the entire party was on the opposite bank. The leader was one of the last to cross. On the bank he stood, crutch under arm, and stubbornly fired in the direction of the concealed enemy until the boat returned on its final trip. But there was trouble for them on both sides of the stream. As they got to horse again and rode off, bullets continued to whine toward them from the trees along their route.[9]

The chase now developed into a race, with the Confederates steadily gaining.[10] At four o'clock in the afternoon they came upon the rear of Dahlgren's column near Bruington Church.[11] The Federals swung about to get on the defensive, and an engagement began in a desultory manner. More Rebels

—home guards and regulars from the Forty-second Virginia
Battalion and the King and Queen Cavalry—came upon the
scene. The firing increased, sparked by some of Pollard's
sharpshooters, ordered to the front.

At last the raiders galloped off in flight. Behind, dead on
the roadside, they left a member of their rear guard. The pur-
suing Confederates searched his pockets, finding a heavy silver
fork bearing the initials J.W.A., a silver watch, a pistol, and
a two-dollar bill someone had attempted to convert into a
fifty.

As darkness came on, Pollard resorted to strategy. Leaving
a few men to continue the chase in a drizzling rain, he struck
off with the others and took a short cut through the countryside, hoping to get ahead of the raiders. Eventually his path
led through the village of Stevensville, and there he picked up
followers, including Edward W. Halbach, the local schoolmaster, and William Littlepage, a thirteen-year-old pupil.
These two trotted along on foot, encouraged by someone
among the riders who said they were going only a short
way.[12]

At Stevensville, Pollard struck the road along which the
raiders would have to come unless they doubled back. There
he turned and went along the River Road toward Walkerton,
near King and Queen Court House, stopped at a point skirted
by the Mattaponi, locally known as Mantapike Hill, and put
his troops in ambush.[13] Two men were sent off to reconnoiter,
and they soon came back with word that the enemy had gone
into camp at Mantapike, just after crossing Anseamancock
Creek.[14]

The halt had been called by Dahlgren to rest and feed his
men and horses. It was their first stop since they had drawn
up for an hour and a half near Short Pump the afternoon
before. Corn was found at a nearby farm. While fires blazed
and food was cooking, the colonel's colored servant took a

few rails from a nearby fence and placed them together on the ground, covering them over with blankets. After eating, Dahlgren stretched out on this makeshift pallet for a brief repose. It would be his last.

When they got back to horse, the young colonel took a place in the second set of fours. Nearby was his next in command, Major Edwin F. Cooke. In the first set, at the young colonel's direction and designed to keep the Confederates from attempting an ambush, was Rebel Captain William F. Dement, one of the officers captured from the court-martial near Frederick's Hall. Farther back was another prisoner, Lieutenant Henry E. Blair of the Salem Artillery. These were the only two captives who had not either escaped or been released.

The column moved slowly at first. Three men had been sent out as pickets nearly three hours before, when the halt first was called, and the advance rode forward expecting to come upon them in the darkness. But no identifying call sounded from the trio, and the riders proceeded with suspicion in their minds that there was unseen trouble waiting for them in this pine-studded, swamp-infested country where Southerners seemed to spring from every point.

Up ahead, Pollard's men waited expectantly.[15] During the long hours since they first had stretched out along the road, they had stared into the darkness and whispered to one another nervously. Some of them were home guards who had seen no battle action, and for them it was a period of great anxiety. As time dragged on, each moment seemed longer.

Around eleven o'clock the Federal column was heard approaching, horses struggling through mud, sabers rattling with every step. The men lying in ambush tensed, their carbines and pistols and ancient muskets ready.

Slowly the column sloshed along. All at once the riders in front stopped. Out of the dark a warning had come to their ears—perhaps an unguarded voice or the click of a rifle trigger. Louis N. Beaudrye of the Fifth New York Cavalry, member of the advance, called out, "Who are you?" At that moment Dahlgren, evidently envisioning some terrorized group of youthful and ancient home guardsmen patriotically nerving themselves to venture beyond their experience, spurred his horse forward and shouted with the impatience of a man accustomed to having his way: "Surrender or I will shoot!" He snapped his pistol as he spoke, and the cap sputtered harmlessly in the dark.

The reaction was instanteous. "A volley was poured in upon us," wrote Beaudrye. "The flash of the pieces afforded us a momentary glimpse of their position stretching parallel with the road about fifteen paces from us. Every tree was occupied, and the bushes poured forth a sheet of fire. A bullet, grazing my leg and probably striking my horse somewhere in the neck, caused him to make a violent spring sideways. I was aware of someone dropping beside me and, attracted by a movement from the ground, demanded who it was. Major Cooke replied that his horse had been shot. Neither of us knew, at the moment, of the death of Dahlgren, though he was not four feet from us when he fell." [16]

Dahlgren's body, found lying in a ditch with the feet against a tree and rail fence bordering the road, had been riddled by five buckshot, all lodged in his back.[17] Dement's horse was down, as dead as Dahlgren, its rider pinned beneath it. The outburst of fire caused a general stampede along the country road—desperate Union soldiers trying blindly to get away from the guns flashing from the bushes.

The pressure in the road increased. Panicked riders doubled back, depending frantically upon the senses of their horses to find an exit. Their junior prisoner, Lieutenant Blair, now on foot, jerked the rails from the fence at one point and opened a gap wide enough for panicky animals to escape, and through it, like sheep bursting from a barnyard, they poured into the field beyond. This was no fortunate choice of ground for the raiders: the field was bordered by the Mattaponi River on one side and, on the other, by a canal that could be crossed at only one place.[18]

Gradually the confusion along the road abated. Those of Dahlgren's men who had managed to escape clung together in the darkness of the nearby field, trying to make as little noise as possible and hoping to devise some method of escape. Dement, who had managed to free himself, made known his identification to the Rebels and was heartily welcomed by them. So was Blair.

Meanwhile Pollard, who had rushed back to the scene from the nearby house, was reacting cautiously. With dozens of hostile Federals running loose in the neighborhood, it seemed to him foolish to drop his guard; so he kept his men at their posts, advising them to remain on the alert and to be ready at daylight to round up all the enemy they could find. A little later, bowing to the rule of military seniority, he turned over the command of his little band of home protectors to Captain Edward C. Fox of the Fifth Virginia Cavalry, newly arrived upon the scene.[19]

With soldiers and home guards held fast to their posts, it was left to William Littlepage, the thirteen-year-old from Stevensville, to grope along the road in search of souvenirs—guns, haversacks, and other items dropped by the raiders in their flight. Stumbling about, he came upon a body.

All his life this youth had longed for a gold watch, and here, in the uniform of this hated enemy lying dead in the mud, might be the end of his rainbow. Unawed by death, he went through the Yankee's pockets. His fingers worked nimbly. He produced a cigar case, a notebook, and some folded papers, and he tucked them into his own clothing.

And then he found a watch! Off he went into the night to locate his schoolmaster.

Unknown to him, the dead man was Ulric Dahlgren and the papers he had taken packed dynamite: in a matter of hours they would have Southerners gasping in horror and anger, and would involve the North and South in a first-class hassle that would continue for generations.

9

"Burn the Hateful City"

THURSDAY, MARCH 3, the fourth day since Kilpatrick had started his ambitious raid toward the Confederate capital, found the excitement over the attack on the city fading. Wild reports still were circulating, and it was difficult to determine which could be relied upon; but for more than twenty-four hours all had been quiet in the outskirts. Yet it was still unknown how completely the Federals had been defeated. Were they in flight, or were they bracing for another assault? Slow communications delayed the answer for a tauntingly long time.

Meanwhile New York papers were whooping it up over Kilpatrick's destruction of railroads leading to Richmond. They were also calculating its effect. Influenced more by bias than sound reasoning, they estimated that at least four weeks would be required to repair the damage. Obviously this constituted a severe blow to Lee, for scouts were unanimous in their reports that his army kept only six to ten days' rations on hand.

Actually, the first effect of the break noticed by the Confederates along the Rapidan and upper Rappahannock was the disruption of contact with the folks back home. Thomas Caffey, a diligent soldier who corresponded so regularly with his sister that he sometimes had to erase the pencil script from her letters in order to supply himself with paper for a reply, informed her at this troublous period: "We have had no mail for some days on account of the Yankees' cavalry getting into our rear and cutting the railroad between Orange and Richmond. We have a line of more than forty miles to guard; and the rascals found out, after a good deal of maneuvering, where our troops were posted, succeeded in flanking us on the right and left, and before we could concentrate our troops they did an immense amount of mischief." But he was certain of the Southern army's invincibility. A rumor was afloat that the Federals were crossing the Rapidan, and for that he had comment: "If this is the case, you may expect to hear of a battle in a few days. We have so many men now at home on furlough that our force is considerably weakened, but we have enough here to wallop all the Yankees Meade can muster up." [1]

In Richmond there was a general tendency to minimize the destruction wrought by the invading columns. Optimistically reported the *Inquirer* the morning of the 3rd: "An assessment of the damage done by the raiders is being slowly made up, from which it would appear that theft was the main object sought to be accomplished in their daring enterprise against the capital of the Confederacy." Prisoners were still coming into the city, and about fifteen Union dead had been buried.

At eight o'clock that morning, a raw, cold day, New Kent Court House, roughly twenty-five miles east of the Confederate capital, trembled to the thud of hostile cavalry. There the combined columns of Kilpatrick and Mitchell merged with the troops Butler had promised to send to that point by three o'clock Wednesday. [2] In all there were 3800 men, two separate detachments led by Colonel Robert W. West, officer in charge at Fort Magruder, and Colonel Samuel F. Spear of the Eleventh Pennsylvania volunteer horse. West had among his troops a brigade of Negroes who marched so well that they drew his praise—forty-two miles in twenty-four hours, a part of the time in a heavy rainstorm and over roads that offered little encouragement to a foot soldier. Spear led the cavalry. He had ridden without halt the first night out, had taken a three-and-a-half-hour rest next morning, and then had gone on to Tunstall's Station on the Richmond & West Point Railroad. There he had destroyed the track, some cars, switches, culverts, depot storehouses, and a large sawmill equipped with a new steam engine that had just ripped out 20,000 feet of lumber.[3] The second night he went into camp at New Kent to await Kilpatrick.

There was great jubilation among the raiders at the sight of Butler's troops. It meant, in effect, a rescue.[4] Now they would be able to rest—their first undisturbed rest since the previous Saturday night—while someone else kept watch against the pestering Rebels. On the morrow the final lap to safety: a march to Williamsburg and thence to Yorktown, to board Federal transports sent to furnish transportation up the Potomac.

With the soldiers would go the contrabands, now making up a group of sizable proportions. And while the soldiers might be worrying over the grilling fights through which they had passed, or that still lay ahead of them, it was a time of jubilation for these colored people. Here and there along the route of Kilpatrick's march they had come running, babbling with glee and excitement, to join the column. Some were young, some old, some with bundles, some bareheaded, and all willing to sacrifice their souls for freedom. Without conscience or reluctance they told where provisions for man or beast were hidden, the location of Rebel pickets and scouts, and when the last Confederate soldier had passed along the road. Loud were their shouts, "Glory! Glory! Hallelujah!"

And they looked back in defiance, crying, "Good-by, Missis, good-by, Marster. We's gwine to be free!" Their cheers at sight of the Negro infantry were terrific, and when the column moved, the advance guard found it difficult to keep them under control.

No one would know what was in Kilpatrick's mind as he drew up at New Kent. His arrival there was in a way further evidence of the complete failure of his undertaking, for it meant he was running to the sheltering arms of Ben Butler, the general whose own abortive effort to release the prisoners in Richmond had been used as an example for the second expedition. It was Wade Hampton who deserved the credit for the predicament in which Kilpatrick found himself. The Federal leader had planned to follow a different route of escape, to get across the Pamunkey and head toward Gloucester Point. And he had made a conscientious effort toward attaining that goal. At Putney's Ferry and again at White House Landing he had stopped and searched diligently for some means of crossing, but Hampton's Confederates had got there ahead of him and either hidden or destroyed the boats.[5]

Another story of frustration was developing along the narrow, winding, muddy roads of King and Queen County, where Dahlgren's pitiful survivors were expecting the worse.[6] Throughout the cold, dark hours of early morning after the leader's death they plotted and schemed in whispers to determine some way of making their escape. Major Cooke, now the ranking officer among them, held a consultation with Signal Officer Bartley and Louis Beaudrye of the Fifth New York Cavalry, one day to be a minister of the Gospel. They believed that they were surrounded by a large force, something like twenty-five miles from Gloucester Point; and under the circumstances it was decided best to dismount and steal away in small groups.

Instructions were relayed in whispers. There was some talk of killing the horses to keep them from falling into the hands

of the Rebels, but the notion was discarded for fear of attracting attention. Instead, sabers were driven into the ground and
the animals picketed to them. Carbines were put out of order
by removing and throwing away the chambers or by breaking
the magazine tubes. Men were cautioned to take only their
belts, revolvers, and haversacks, for any excess luggage they
might be forced to abandon along the way would point to
their trail and assist pursuit.

Despite the decision and the preparations, when the time
came to move off only a minority were eager to depart. Most
of the men shivering there in the darkness felt that to flee
would be foolish—a certain way to bring about personal destruction. They thought that these relentless Southerners,
whose voices they had listened to since the ambush just before
midnight, would hunt them down with dogs and mete out
the same rough treatment their dead leader had received. So
at daylight many were waiting in Gresham's field to surrender.

But off into the darkness before dawn went dozens of the
hardier and more determined. Twenty-one of them, including Dahlgren's Negro body servant, were destined to make
good their escape.

Cooke, Bartley, and Beaudrye moved away together, creep-
ing on hands and knees for half a mile before they straightened
and walked normally. At daylight they crawled into a jungle
of young pines, flopped exhaustedly, and tried to sleep. Hours
later, as darkness again approached, they resumed their journey. Along the way they met up with others, and the group
numbered six when they eventually stopped at a cabin in the
hope of procuring food. It turned out to be the home of an
aged plantation overseer named McFarland. He threw back
the door in welcome, surprising them with his cordiality.
Waving invitingly toward a large fire blazing on the hearth,
he called to his wife to prepare them a meal, and then he
hustled about, apparently looking to their welfare. But only
grief was to be found beneath his roof. While the raiders

relaxed around the fireplace, a Negro girl stole out on a mission that brought bursting into the room a handful of drawling Southerners, all armed to the teeth.

The leader of these intruders, it developed, was the owner of the plantation, Captain Richard Hugh Bagby, pastor of a nearby Baptist church and one of the embattled Confederates who had stopped Dahlgren. With the others he had come in from beating the bushes, and was on the verge of sitting down to dinner when the servant brought word that some of the men he was hunting now rested only a few yards away.

Under his direction the prisoners were marched up to the big house. The festive board in the dining room was extended to meet the demand, and both captors and captives sat down together, the former with weapons at their elbows. Major Cooke, in particular, was impressed by the gun-toting, Bible-pounding host; and he recorded that while they bowed their heads in supplication, the minister intoned words of grace, cocked revolver in hand.

Despite the display of armament around the room, it was a genial occasion. The meal was eaten with the unhurried grace of a plantation dinner and, when all the food was gone, the prisoners, warmed and comfortable, were allowed to blanket down on the floor. They slept that night under guard. The next day they would be on their way to Richmond, to Libby, and past the mound of dirt covering the dreaded "torpedo." [7]

Meanwhile Dahlgren, in death, was still proving a live issue. The home guardsmen who had gathered around his body the night he fell made no effort to disperse. Throughout the miserable hours they waited, rolled in blankets or snuggled down in a cover of pine branches. Still among them were Halbach and his pupil, William Littlepage, and as they bedded together in a woody bivouac the boy passed over to his teacher the cigar case, notebook, and folded papers he had taken from the dead man's pockets. But not the watch.

Dawn came slowly. It was a dark and dreary day, and the

night mists that had crept in through the trees now hung low in the bushes, like smoke caught under an umbrella. Halbach took out the notebook and papers and scanned them. The more he read, the angrier he became.[8]

Copied in ink on one of the folded papers, a sheet of the official Third Division stationery, was Dahlgren's address to the troops under his command. In flowery language he exhorted them to "write your names on the hearts of your countrymen in letters that can never be erased." They were to release the prisoners on Belle Isle first, after which the liberated men were to be encouraged to "destroy and burn the hateful city." Then came the additional instruction: "Do not allow the Rebel leader Davis and his traitorous crew to escape." [9]

On a similar sheet, also in ink, without salutation and without signature, were the detailed orders prepared for Mitchell, to aid him in leading the separate detachment down the north bank of the James. Dahlgren left no doubts about what should be done in Richmond: "The bridges will be burned and the city destroyed. The men must keep together and well in hand, and once in the city it must be destroyed and Jeff. Davis and Cabinet killed." There were other instructions that stirred Halbach's blood: "Horses and cattle which we do not need immediately must be shot rather than left . . . Men will stop at Bellona Arsenal and totally destroy it, and everything else but hospitals . . . Everything on the canal and elsewhere of service to the Rebels must be destroyed."

A third sheet of the official stationery bore an early itinerary that directed the departure from Stevensburg on the night of the 27th, twenty-four hours before it actually took place. The memorandum book, bearing on its first page Dahlgren's signature and apparent date of purchase, revealed that he had done much idle planning while waiting at Kilpatrick's headquarters for the raid to begin. There were many characteristic jottings in pencil, some of them hastily made, with interlineations and corrections. Some of these notations had been incorporated in the address and in Mitchell's instructions. The reference to Jefferson Davis and Cabinet was accompanied by the additional directive that they "must be killed on the spot." Also in the booklet was a rough draft in pencil of Dahlgren's address to his men. It differed somewhat from the copy written in ink, for there was much interlining, one instance of which stated: "You must encourage the prisoners to destroy the city; make one vast flame of it."

Other papers included the letter from the Provost Marshal General's Office identifying Martin Robinson. It was marked "Confidential." Another was a folded facsimile of a hundred-dollar bill issued by the "Plantation Bank" and good for one bottle of "Plantation Bitters."

Frequently during the morning Halbach exhibited these papers to officers and others. Some urged that they be destroyed at once, warning that if he were captured with them on his person he would be shot. But the teacher was stubborn and thoroughly angry. Why destroy written evidence that showed beyond question the attitude and thinking that had steered this raid into Rebel territory?

While Halbach pondered his find, the pursuit of Dahlgren's scattered column was proving highly successful. The men who had opposed flight were found waiting in the field near Mantapike Hill amid a scene of confusion—scattered arms, saddles, haversacks, canteens, utensils, blankets. Ninety-two officers and privates, thirty-eight contrabands, and a number of horses were in the group. As the prisoners were rounded up, a wide assortment of loot, most of it silverware, was discovered in their pockets and saddle bags: knives, forks, spoons, coffee and tea pots, sugar dishes, salvers. Much of this would find its way back to the rightful owners.

But none of the prisoners professed to know anything about the papers found on their leader's body. Even Hogan, the scout, repeatedly denied under pressure that he was aware of their existence.[10]

At two o'clock in the afternoon, while trying to overtake more of Dahlgren's men, Halbach came up with Lieutenant Pollard and exhibited the papers to him. Until that time Pollard had known nothing of their existence.[11] He showed growing excitement as he read, and in the end he asked the schoolmaster to let him take them to Richmond. Halbach was reluctant at first—he knew quite as well as anyone what to do with them—but at last he was induced by friends to consent, on the argument that in Pollard's hands they would reach the Confederate capital much quicker than by the semiweekly mail.

Later in the day, at Old Church, Pollard found the commanding officer of the Ninth Virginia Cavalry, Colonel R. L. T. Beale, and turned over to him the papers, memorandum book, and Dahlgren's wooden leg. The colonel examined them carefully and then, retaining the notebook, directed the lieutenant to take the other items to Wade Hampton or, if that general could not be located, to Fitzhugh Lee.

As Pollard picked his way through the night over a route to Richmond well known to him, a report of Kilpatrick's progress was on its way to Washington. At the same time, from Fort Magruder, Butler relayed a message to Secretary of War Stanton. It announced that the raiders had reached that point, but not without certain important losses: Dahlgren and Cooke were supposed to be prisoners and Litchfield either wounded or killed.

An hour or so later Kilpatrick sent off a dispatch in cipher to Pleasonton. It was the first report he had made of his progress since the triumphant message scribbled from Ely's Ford early Monday morning. It was far different in tone from its predecessor:

"I have reached General Butler's lines with my command in good order. I have failed to accomplish the great object of the expedition, but have destroyed the enemy's communications at various points on the Virginia Central Railroad; also the canal and mills along the James River, and much other valuable property. Drove the enemy into and through his fortifications to the suburbs of Richmond; made several unsuccessful efforts to return to the Army of the Potomac. I have lost less than one hundred and fifty men. The entire command is in good order, and needs but a few days' rest. I respectfully ask for instructions."

By this time the excited activity around Mantapike Hill had waned to an occasional visit of local residents drawn by curiosity to the spot where Dahlgren lay buried. Without ceremony the body had been placed in a shallow grave—"in a slashy, muddy hole at the fork of two roads, one leading from Stevensville, the other from Mantua Ferry," reported Betty Van Lew. The soldiers and home guards who served as gravediggers and pallbearers had expressed little but anger and abuse as they proceeded with their chores. This was the general tenor of opinion except in the minds of Dement and Blair, the Confederates who had been rescued at the time of the Yankee colonel's downfall. In their hearts these two despised Dahlgren's purposes, but they admitted that he had attracted their admiration as a dashing soldier and a man of polish and education. They revealed he had shared his rations with them and treated them with all courtesy and consideration.[12] Moreover, neither the leader nor his men had mentioned in their presence the vicious objectives of the raid as revealed by the written evidence.

10

Coffin and Headboard, at Least

Tʜᴇ ɴᴇᴡs ᴏɴ Fʀɪᴅᴀʏ ᴍᴏʀɴɪɴɢ, March 4, was good at Union General George G. Meade's headquarters. Scouts sent across the Rapidan in search of intelligence had come back with much to tell, bringing with them the lone agent dispatched the previous week to cut the telegraph lines at Frederick's Hall. He had accomplished his mission at eleven o'clock Sunday night, just as Dahlgren was crossing at Ely's Ford. Taken prisoner later, he spent several hours in the hands of the Rebels before making his escape near Chancellorsville, and while a captive he was told of important developments, all hearsay, including the capture of General Lee. But the scout's report was soon outdated. Dispatches arrived by noon that completely changed the story, and Meade wired Kilpatrick to proceed to Yorktown and there await further orders.

Dahlgren's fate at this time was still unknown to his fellow officers. A Rebel deserter reported that a one-legged colonel and about a hundred men had been taken prisoner, and Kilpatrick wired Butler that he still had hopes that the leader

of his advance column would come in.¹ Abraham Lincoln
was so notified.

Northern newspapers relayed conflicting reports on the
progress of the raid. Most of them apparently knew nothing
they could not have passed on to the public Wednesday
morning, but the New York *Times* was an exception. This
journal was able to interview some of the survivors and learn
that the expedition was far from a success. Its failure seemed
to rest upon Martin Robinson, the Negro guide, and the
reporter who did the interviewing was unable to refrain from
a bit of editorializing: "The man who thus dared to trifle
with the welfare of his country, when it became evident that
one of the most important objects would prove a failure
through his willful connivance, was immediately hanged upon
the spot; thus meeting a fate he so richly deserved." ²

In Confederate circles there was rising jubilation. Reported
Richmond's *Daily Dispatch:* "The injury to the communications of the Army of Northern Virginia can be repaired in
three days, and instead of releasing the prisoners already in
our hands, they have added not less than two hundred and
fifty to their numbers." And on the banks of the South Anna,
where the raiders' trail had crossed, a band of citizens and
soldiers chuckled as they worked. Out of the muddy waters
of this stream they were dragging a ton or more of ammunition dumped by the Federals. Hundreds of cartridges suited
to Burnside rifles, as well as thousands of pounds of other
types, were coming to the surface.³

Early that morning Wade Hampton, who had spent the
night at the home of Dr. Braxton, extended thanks to his host
and rode on his way, along the most direct route from King
and Queen to Richmond. Soon he met one of the distinguished residents of the neighborhood, patriarch Lewis Washington. The old fellow was excited. He told the cavalry leader
a courier was in search of him, had stopped at the Washington
manor overnight, and now was on his way to the Confederate

capital with papers that told of the entire diabolical plan of the Union raid.

This courier was Pollard. Later in the day, unable to find Hampton, he came into Richmond and hurried to the office of Fitzhugh Lee, finding him seated with Jeb Stuart's doughty warrior, Heros von Borcke, on leave in the capital while recuperating from wounds.[4] Producing the papers and the artificial leg, the lieutenant from the Ninth Virginia told his story. Lee and the German were greatly interested and examined the trophies carefully. A few minutes later Lee hurried to show them to Jefferson Davis, interrupting a conference with Confederate Secretary of State Judah P. Benjamin. The President read the papers aloud, laughing over the statement, "Jeff Davis and Cabinet must be killed." [5]

"That means you, Mr. Benjamin," he chuckled.

When he had finished scanning the papers, the President directed that they be taken to Sam Cooper, the Adjutant General, to be filed. Lee carried out instructions, passing them along with the observation: "They need no comment." [6] Back at Lee's office, meanwhile, the wooden leg was being handed about with much curiosity. It soon would go on display in a Richmond store window, and later it would be turned over as a model to army surgeons.[7]

But the papers were not to drop out of sight into a niche in Adjutant General files. Before the day ended they were perused by Davis' military adviser, General Braxton Bragg, whose reaction was grave and completely unlike that of the President. "It has occurred to me," he wrote the Secretary of War, "that the papers just captured from the enemy are of such an extraordinary and diabolical character that some more formal method should be adopted of giving them to the public than simply lending them to the press. My own conviction is for an execution of the prisoners and a publication as justification; but in any event the publication should go forth with official sanction from the highest authority, calling the attention of our people and the civilized world to the fiendish and atrocious conduct of our enemies." [8]

General Josiah Gorgas, the South's masterful ordnance officer, read them, too, and was so stirred by them that he made an entry in his diary: "Today were captured Colonel Dahlgren and his command of raiders—outlaws—bandits. He was dead, but on his body were found the orders to his command, which were to enter the city, set it on fire in as many places as possible, liberate the prisoners, capture and kill the President and his Cabinet, and to commit every possible horror on the Capital. What beasts and murderers. Hereafter those that are taken will not be heard of." [9]

The Richmond *Whig* appeared with an editorial: "Are these men warriors? Are they soldiers, taken in the performance of duties recognized as legitimate by the loosest construction in the code of civilized warfare? Or are they assassins, barbarians, thugs who have forfeited (and expect to lose) their lives? Are they not barbarians redolent with more hellish purposes than were the Goth, the Hun or the Saracen?"

The South's anger built. And meanwhile not all was roses for Kilpatrick, either north or south of the Potomac. Another diarist, one Marsena R. Patrick, provost marshal general of the Army of the Potomac, closed out the date with an entry that showed he personally was not among the raid leader's most ardent admirers: "Kilpatrick has been heard from at Yorktown. He has done nothing but drive in the pickets to Richmond. Probably gave notice of his proximity to the Capitol by his fight at Hanover Junction, which should have been avoided." [10]

And in the closing hours of the day a message from headquarters was brought to the home guard valiantly standing watch along the sloppy roads of King and Queen: Dahlgren's body must be exhumed and brought to Richmond immediately "for the purpose of identification."

This message put an end to operations that would have

pleased Scout Christopher Hogan. When rounded up with other prisoners in the field off Mantapike Hill, he had pleaded for a decent burial for Dahlgren. A coffin and headboard at least, he begged. And some of his captors, Halbach among them, agreed. The teacher did not signify his approval by words alone. Soon he was busy preparing a neat little headboard with the name of the dead carved in readable letters. The messenger from Richmond arrived while they were in the midst of transferring the body to a coffin and more decent grave.[11]

11

"Kill Has Dished Himself"

THE STORM BORN of William Littlepage's pocket-rifling reached its peak on Saturday, March 5, a clear and pleasant day. That morning Richmond newspapers reported with flaming headlines the contents of Ulric Dahlgren's papers. They also told in detail, with due praise to Lieutenant Pollard, a kinsman of one of the local editors, of the ambush near Walkerton and of the capture next morning of prisoners and horses. Said the *Examiner:* "The wretch who commanded them was the son of Commodore Dahlgren, of ordnance notoriety. It would have been well if the body of the land pirate had been gibbeted in chains on the spot where he fell." [1]

The *Examiner*'s article was clipped out by none other than the South's Secretary of War, James Seddon, whose wife had been a sweetheart of the senior Dahlgren and who had chatted and sipped wine from the silver goblets with "Little Ully" the day before his death. Seddon cut the clipping to attach to a letter he was writing General Robert E. Lee. He thought at least a part of the prisoners captured in King and Queen should be executed, and, noting that "General Bragg's views coincide with my own on this subject," Seddon was writing to get Lee's views. "You will, of course, appreciate to what consequences such a course may not rightfully, yet not unnaturally, considering the unscrupulousness and malignity of our foes, lead, and estimate such results in forming your judgment," he concluded.[2]

The *Examiner* did not stand alone in its grave opinion of the written evidence William Littlepage had discovered. The *Dispatch* was editorializing too. "Decidedly we think," its columns stated, "that these Dahlgren papers will destroy, during the rest of this war, all rose-water chivalry; and that Confederate armies will make war after and upon the rules selected by their enemies."

The full extent of the threat that the Union raid had brought upon Richmond was now clear to the city's residents. Much of the population was made up of refugee women and children whose menfolk were off fighting in the armies. People shuddered to think what might have happened if the thousands of half-starved prisoners shut up on Belle Isle—the "scrapings and rakings of Europe," Union General Neal Dow had called them—had been turned loose in the Rebel capital.

Even Mrs. Chesnut, usually a calm woman, was shaken by thought of the calamity that might have been inflicted. She was walking home with gentlemanly Tom Ferguson and heard the story of Dahlgren's death and of the "horrid tablets" found in his pocket. Armed with this pulse-stirring news, she went over to visit her neighbor, Mrs. Semmes, and found this astute lady covering her lettuce and radishes as blissfully as if the Yankee raiders were a myth. But not to Mrs. Chesnut: "And to think, here I sat reading 'Romola' at my ease, and I might have been roused at any moment by fire and fury, rapine and murder."

Many people were in favor of executing Dahlgren's men, but temperance ruled War Clerk Jones in his daily record of what was happening in the Confederate capital. Referring to the "memoranda" from the raid, he reported that "the Cabinet have been in consultation many hours in regard to it, and I have reason to believe it is the present purpose to deal summarily with the captives taken with Dahlgren, but the 'sober second thought' will prevail, and they will not be executed, notwithstanding the thunders of the press. Retaliation for such outrages committed on others having been declined, the President and Cabinet can hardly be expected to begin with such sanguinary punishments when their own lives are threatened. It would be an act liable to grave criticism." Then he took note of Secretary Seddon's letter to General Lee and commented: "We shall soon know, I hope, what General Lee will have to say on the subject, and I am mistaken if he does not oppose it. If these men had been put to death in the heat of passion, on the field, it would have been justified, but it is too late now. Besides, Gen. Lee's son is a captive in the hands of the enemy, designated for retaliation whenever we shall execute any of their prisoners in our hands. It is cruelty to Gen. Lee!" [3]

Union headquarters was fast to learn of the outcome of Kilpatrick's venture, but slower in hearing of Dahlgren's fate. Yet, while the raid would eventually be dubbed a failure officially, to the public it still seemed a partial success for the wreckage and plunder left in its wake.[4] In his official report Kilpatrick had said, "It is impossible to estimate the amount of property destroyed and damage done to the enemy during this raid." But one development on March 5 would do much to discount the importance of Kilpatrick's accomplishments: the rail connections with Lee's army that the raiders were supposed to have put out of order for "at least three weeks" was returned to full running order. As Thomas Caffey, the faithful letter-writer in camp along the Rapidan, announced to his sister the following day: "The train from Richmond came through yesterday for the first time since the Yankee raid, and a very heavy mail for the regiment was received." [5]

Back at Brandy Station, Colonel Theodore Lyman, Meade's sarcastic aide, recorded in his diary: "Behold my prophecy in regard to Kilcavalry's raid fulfilled. I have heard many persons very indignant with him. They said he went to the President and pressed his plan; told Pleasanton he would not come back alive if he didn't succeed; that he is a frothy braggart, without brains and not overstocked with desire to fall on the field; and that he gets all his reputation by newspapers and political influence. These charges are not new and I fancy Kill has rather dished himself. It is painful to think of these poor prisoners hearing the sound of his guns and hoping a rescue was at hand! Now all that cavalry must be carried back in steamers, like a parcel of old women going to market!" [6]

Lyman knew whereof he wrote, for he had seen copies of messages flashing back and forth between Butler, Kilpatrick, and headquarters. At the moment the raiders were under orders to divide into two groups, one to board transports at Yorktown, the other at Newport News. [7]

The New York *Herald*, whose correspondent wrote from headquarters, reported that it was feared the raid had not been successful, and fixed the blame primarily upon premature publication of the movement by Republican newspapers. Chief of Staff Humphrey and Provost Marshal General Patrick were said to be investigating the matter.

But the storm of criticism broke in full fury on Sunday, when it was definitely known by certain Union authorities that Ulric Dahlgren was as dead as Rebel bullets could make him. Meade that day received a copy of Saturday's Richmond *Sentinel*, read it, and prepared to send it to Halleck, with the comment: "I fear the account is true."

Then he wrote his wife: "You have doubtless seen that Kilpatrick's raid was an utter failure. I did not expect much from it. Poor Dahlgren I am sorry for." [8]

To Pleasanton on this day Kilpatrick sent a report from Yorktown in which he was obviously trying to conceal the utter failure of the expedition. "I left my camp at Stevensburg with three thousand five hundred and eighty-four men, six guns, eight caissons, three wagons, and six ambulances. I have now three thousand and seventeen men, three thousand five hundred and ninety-five horses, six guns, eight caissons, three wagons and four ambulances." While the figure that would show the total loss of horses was omitted, intentionally or otherwise, Kilpatrick's count of his current strength was far from accurate. And so was other information contained in the message. It told that Colonel Dahlgren, with about a hundred men, "has been heard from today; he was then near King and Queen Court House." This was nearly four days after Dahlgren had been ambushed and killed!

The "news" regarding the young colonel was relayed from Kilpatrick to Abraham Lincoln by General Butler. Butler added that a rescue force was on its way. This rescue was to be made by the gunboat *Morse*, already on its way from Yorktown.[9]

In the meantime the Confederates, their home guard joining in with regular army, were stretching their lines in an effort to head off Kilpatrick if he tried to get back to Washington by land. To watch for such a development, Wade Hampton had stationed troops at Fredericksburg and all the way across the Northern Neck.

During the day Lee was heard from, and his reply was a corroboration of War Clerk Jones' estimate. The Confederate leader concurred with Seddon that the Dahlgren papers should be formally and officially published, in order that the world might know "the unchristian and atrocious acts" the enemy plotted. But he said that he could not recommend execution of the prisoners. He pointed out that the papers revealed only the intentions of Dahlgren, that the plans had not been executed, and that it was not known whether they had been imparted to his soldiers or that they were sanctioned by the Federal government. "I think it better to do right," he advised, "even if we suffer in so doing, than to incur the reproach of our consciences and posterity." To execute the men, he reminded, "would produce retaliation. How many and better men have we in the enemy's hands than they have in ours?" he asked. And then he added: "But this consideration should have no weight provided the course was in itself right. Yet history records instances where such considerations have prevented the execution of marauders and devastators of provinces."

In the afternoon Lieutenant Christian of Company H, Ninth Virginia Cavalry, leading an escort of only half a dozen or so men, arrived by train at the York River Railroad station in Richmond, thus completing an unpleasant assignment. It was his duty to see that Dahlgren's body arrived safely in the Rebel capital.

When the train stopped, Christian and his detail were gathered in the baggage car beside a plain white pine coffin. In a short while there arrived Captain Dement and others who had seen Dahlgren before his death. The lid was removed. Then they stood around the box and stared down at its contents. The body, one viewer recorded, "was decidedly more genteel than could be expected, considering the length of time he has been dead." It was dressed in cotton shirt and dark pants, and wrapped in a military blanket.[10] A *Dispatch* reporter wrote that the dead man's countenance "indicated that of pain," and the *Whig* correspondent went a bit further and said "his face wore an expression of agony." It was noticed that the body had two extremities missing: the right leg and the little finger of the left hand, the latter severed by someone back in the swamp-infested countryside of King and Queen County to get a ring that would not come off otherwise.[11]

12

"Like a Parcel of Old Women"

Early the morning of March 7 the gunboat *Morse*, steered to the directions of the enterprising Lieutenant Commander Babcock, swung up past West Point, where the Pamunkey and Mattaponi flow together to form the York. There it veered to the right, along the latter tributary, in the direction of King and Queen Court House, firing its signal gun at intervals in the hope of attracting some of the desperate Union refugees. At seven o'clock the crew heard shouting offshore on the starboard side, and soon a small boat could be seen putting out from an inlet, its oars handled by a stocky Negro. In a few minutes four of Dahlgren's horsemen and his colored body servant were helped aboard. The soldiers were relieved to be among friends again, and they had many nice things to say about the man who had done the rowing, a freedman who had furnished them with both guidance and transportation.

In a matter of hours a report of the rescue was on its way to Gideon Welles, Union Secretary of the Navy. It was signed by Samuel Phillips Lee, acting rear admiral of the

North Atlantic Blockading Squadron, and it told that Dahl-gren was dead. This news, Lee said, came from none other than Dahlgren's servant, who related that he had seen his colonel's naked corpse lying alongside the road, the ring-finger severed.[1]

While this rescue was in progress, back in Richmond a long line of curious people continued to pass the white pine box in which lay Dahlgren's body. Many heaped abuse upon the still form. "Shocking to decency was the talk over the corpse," reported the Union spy, Betty Van Lew, among the few sympathetic souls to move past the bier.[2] This procession continued through the morning and into the afternoon. At two o'clock a detail of soldiers led by Lieutenant Colonel John Wilder Atkinson, commanding the First Division of Richmond defense troops, appeared at the railway station with a four-mule street wagon and prepared to carry out orders said to have come from Jefferson Davis himself. The lid of the coffin, with the name "Ulric Dahlgren" stenciled across it, was put back in place and fastened with screws. Then the box was lifted into the wagon, and the vehicle, escorted by the guard under Atkinson, moved toward the outskirts of the city. Bystanders noted it was going in the direction of Oakwood Cemetery, where usually were buried prisoners who died in hospitals in the eastern part of the city. No one was allowed to follow, and War Clerk Jones merely recorded in his diary that the body was "transferred to some retired burial place." He also noted that Secretary of War Seddon had gone up to his farm for a few days to see the extent of damage done him by the enemy's destructive visit to the neighborhood.

Next morning the *Whig* was as uninformative as Clerk Jones about the disposition of Dahlgren's body: "About two o'clock P.M. the corpse was removed from the depot and buried—no one knows, or is to know, where."

The *Examiner* said a little more, and with fire: "Henceforth the name of Dahlgren is linked with eternal infamy, and in the years to come defenseless women and innocent childhood will peruse, with a sense of shrinking horror, the story of Richmond's rescue from the midnight sack and ravage led by Dahlgren." Then it told of the treatment accorded his corpse, of how it had been stripped and tossed in a field to save it from the hogs roaming about King and Queen County. As for the burial, it said in conclusion: "Yesterday afternoon the body was removed from the car that brought it to the York River Railroad Depot and given to the spot of earth selected to receive it. Where that spot is no one but those concerned in its burial know or care to tell. It was a dog's burial, without coffin, winding sheet or service. Friends and relatives at the North need inquire no further; this is all they will know—he is buried, a burial that befitted the mission upon which he came. He has 'swept through the city of Richmond' on a pine bier and 'written his name' on the scroll of infamy, instead of 'on the hearts of his countrymen,' never to be erased. He 'asked the blessing of Almighty God' on his mission of rapine, murder and blood, and the Almighty cursed him instead."

The *Dispatch* had still a different idea. "The only use to which we can practically devote the remains of the dead," wrote its editor, "is to employ them with some moral advantage to the living. We bury with ceremony and pomp the great and good, and mark their resting place with a tomb of enduring material, on which we inscribe some account of their virtues for the admiration and emulation of future generations. Why may we not derive a beneficial lesson from a monument of an opposite character? Suppose Dahlgren to be buried in a prominent place, and that a stone should be set up over it simply and briefly stating that there he was and who he was. It should be a monument of infamy—a beacon to warn all of the fate of one so execrable."

Such a condemnation of the dead son of one of the Union's

top admirals would hardly make friends in the North. Nor would the notice in the Richmond press that the officers captured from Kilpatrick's command were to be put in irons.[3] Both of these announcements were seen by Ben Butler, and he immediately sent off letters of protest to Judge Robert Ould, Confederate Commissioner of Exchange. A letter concerning Dahlgren requested that his body be returned to his family.[4]

By Tuesday, Kilpatrick was brought up to date on developments, and at last became resigned to Dahlgren's fate. Back to Yorktown had steamed the *Morse*, bringing in twelve refugees, among them the Negro body servant.

Now all at once there was vengeance in the hearts of the Union command at Yorktown, and thoughts were concentrated on the execution of a retaliatory thrust in force upon King and Queen Court House. Just who masterminded the expedition somehow was lost in the excitement of the moment, but both Butler and Kilpatrick claimed credit. Butler said he sent the troops "to deal with those citizens who, claiming to be non-combatants when any force of ours is there, yet turned out and ambushed Dahlgren." [5] Kilpatrick, in an equally formal report, said "the outrageous treatment of the remains of Colonel Dahlgren and the cruel and barbarous manner in which his men were hunted down and captured by citizens and soldiers with dogs determined me to visit the neighborhood of King and Queen Court House with a sufficient force to punish those who had been engaged in the murder of Colonel Dahlgren and the capture of his men." [6]

Regardless of who instigated the plan, Brigadier General Wistar, the same man who had failed in Butler's early-February attack on Richmond, was in command, and he had an ingenious idea about the best way to get revenge. Two hundred of his cavalry had just come back from King and Queen, where they had been hounded mile after mile by small bands of Rebel horsemen. Wistar decided to set a trap, to move his infantry in by transports at night, and to station it along the main road at least twelve hours before the arrival at dawn of the cavalry, which was moving by land. As the Rebel bands fell back before the advancing Kilpatrick, the Union infantry would be in position to intercept them.

At three o'clock on Wednesday morning, the 9th, Kilpatrick was dispatched from Gloucester Point with 700 of Wistar's cavalry and about 400 of his own.[7] His instructions were to move by easy stages and to arrive and communicate with the infantry at Sheppard's Landing near King and Queen Court House at—and not before—dawn. But it was noticed as these soldiers rode into the night that Kilpatrick was not among them. They were led by Colonel Addison W. Preston, commanding the Second Brigade.

During the early afternoon, while the cavalry was making its way up the peninsula, Wistar moved his troops aboard transports at Yorktown. Twenty-seven hundred men filed up the gangplanks—Sam Duncan's brigade and Joe Kiddoo's Twenty-second Regiment U.S. Colored Troops. Then up York River swung the string of ships, escorted as far as West Point by three gunboats. On board one of the three was Kilpatrick.

At eight-thirty that night, after grounding once or twice on its way up the Mattaponi, the convoy arrived at Sheppard's Landing. The ships worked slowly in toward shore in the dark; the wharf was hastily repaired; and the troops landed, all in fine shape and all according to schedule.

But Wistar's ingenious plans were doomed to disappointment. Preston had ridden through the country much faster than expected, and was at that moment bivouacked on the main road, just where the Union infantry was supposed to lie in wait for the retiring Rebels.

In the face of this development, Wistar directed Kilpatrick to move with all the cavalry before daylight to King and

Queen, destroy the courthouse and public buildings, and especially the ferry near that place, and to meet him at a crossroads about six miles away. At ten o'clock that morning Wistar arrived at the rendezvous to find Kilpatrick had stopped with his cavalry at Plymouth and had sent forward Wistar's cavalry under Colonel Benny Onderdonk to do the burning.

"Being disappointed in every way," Wistar reported, he now sent Kilpatrick off on an exploratory expedition along the peninsula, with instructions to meet him next day at Old Dragon Bridge. This put the thoroughly fatigued "Kil-cavalry," a man who at the moment was sick of raiding, of relentless Rebel horsemen, and of the muck and mire of country roads, in the neighborhood of the Dragon, a swampy, muddy, difficult stream, with clayey banks, all winding through dense woods and nowhere spanned by bridges. To make matters worse, one of the steady, soaking eastern Virginia downpours began to fall, and it was not many hours before a courier from the cavalry leader came along searching for Wistar. From his dripping uniform the messenger took a note that told that the Rebels had been routed by Onderdonk. With this assignment completed and reported, Kilpatrick concluded: "I had the honor to report to you yesterday the condition of my command, as well as my objections to further operations in the enemy's country. It will take the best part of a day to repair the bridge; the stream cannot be forded, and with the roads in their present condition my command cannot make a long march. I am ready to move, and await instructions." [8]

Kilpatrick obviously had had his fill, and this Wistar finally recognized. He sent word for the cavalry leader to proceed directly to Yorktown. This particular order apparently was carried out with dispatch, for when Wistar himself returned, Kilpatrick already had left for Washington.

Before leaving, Kilpatrick prepared a report, hurried and

not too explicit, and forwarded it to Butler. It consisted of only two paragraphs, the first of which stated: "My cavalry has returned. The people about King and Queen Court House have been well punished for the murder of Colonel Dahlgren." [9]

Punishment for the Southerners had been concentrated at the courthouse. There almost the entire village was burned, the Richmond *Dispatch* reporting that only one dwelling was left standing.[10] The newspaper termed the destruction "an act of deliberate devilishness on the part of the Yankees." In summing up their casualties, the Confederates could account for only nine soldiers taken prisoner, three of them sergeants.[11] But Wistar reported fifty-odd captives, identifying half of them, however, as citizens.

Kilpatrick got aboard a transport on Saturday, the 12th. He faced another rough period in his life. The immediate task was to pick up the pieces, to resume the regular routine of war he had left behind at Stevensburg. Within a few hours he stepped onto the wharf at Alexandria. There he learned that the remainder of his command, moved upstream a thousand at a time, had been supplied with rations at the Soldiers' Relief and now was bivouacked in the suburbs. It was planned to give the men a few days' rest before marching them back to camp, but this idea was abandoned after one of the Michigan soldiers hacked up a Negro sentry on the streets of Alexandria. To avoid further trouble the return was started without delay.

By the 18th of March—nineteen days after the excitement and suspense with which had begun the raid that was to be "the grandest thing on record"—all of those who survived were back in the camps around Brandy Station and Culpeper and Stevensburg. The undertaking was finally and definitely finished.

But the aftermath caused by it was far from ended. The youthful Ulric had been "tumbled over," and his body was still lying in enemy territory. Worse still, somewhere back there in the hands of the Confederates were the sensational papers taken from his pockets. The raid could not be considered officially concluded so long as these were a subject of controversy.

13

Peach Trees Cover the Dead

THE UNION WAITED for no official protest from
the Confederate government before starting an investigation
of the Dahlgren papers. Even while some of Kilpatrick's men
were on their way back to camp, Meade, desiring to get at
"the truth of this matter," ordered that officers and men be
questioned carefully in an effort to find out whether the address had been given to Dahlgren's command, or even to a
portion of it.[1]

The result was reported by Kilpatrick. He said that he
had examined officers and privates who accompanied Dahlgren
and all testified that no address such as that published in the
Richmond papers had been delivered before them.

Kilpatrick went further: "Colonel Dahlgren, one hour before we separated at my headquarters, handed me an address
that he intended to read to his command. That paper was
indorsed in red ink, 'Approved,' over my official signature.
The alleged address of Colonel Dahlgren published in the
papers is the same as the one approved by me, save so far as it
speaks of *exhorting the prisoners to destroy and burn the*

hateful city and kill the traitor Davis and his Cabinet.' All
this is false and published only as an excuse for the barbarous
treatment of the remains of a brave soldier." [2]

Such from Kilpatrick was not evidence enough: John
Mitchell, second in command to Dahlgren, was called to
headquarters. Then inquiry was made whether or not the
original instructions for the raid, prepared by Meade and
relayed through Pleasanton to Kilpatrick, had been delivered.
Pleasanton had the answer to this: "General Kilpatrick duly
received and acknowledged the instructions of the major
general commanding in reference to the late expedition against
Richmond." [3]

While the investigation was under way, a report of losses
suffered during the venture was assembled, and some of its figures were astounding. Nine officers, 331 men, and 583 horses
had been lost. Four hundred and eighty of the animals that
managed to make it back were put out of service by sore
backs and overexertion. Property losses were disproportion-
ately larger: 90 Spencer rifles, 59 Spencer carbines, 338
Sharps carbines, 107 Burnside carbines, and 516 Colt army
pistols had been left behind somewhere along the mud and
blood-spattered route. So had 505 cavalry sabers, 207 saddles,
432 horse equipments, and other items in equal numbers,
among them overcoats, blankets, ponchos, cartridge boxes,
canteens, haversacks, and pistol holsters.

Many of the losses, especially the horses, were a boon to
the South. In inflated Confederate currency, they represented
thousands upon thousands of dollars.

By March 22, off from Richmond to the Confederacy's
French representative in Paris, John Slidell, went a letter from
Secretary of State Benjamin. It told of the raid, terming it
"as silly as it was desperate," and said that it would deserve
no notice "but for the revelation of the infamous character of
the warfare waged against us." The papers found on Dahlgren, wrote Benjamin, "disclose purposes so foul that the

Northern newspapers, which, prior to the news of his failure, were indulging in their usual boasts of the intended sack of the city, have since endeavored to throw suspicion on the published copies of the papers by alleging that the passage which ordered the President and the Cabinet to be killed had been interpolated here."

The letter continued: "The conclusive answer to this statement will be found in the photographic copies of these papers which are now being executed at the Engineers' Bureau, and which will be forwarded to you by the next mail.[4] If we had anticipated the denial, the copies would have been in time to accompany this dispatch. The papers found on Dahlgren's body were brought to Richmond by the courier who was dispatched from the scene of the conflict in which Dahlgren was killed, and I happened to be in conference with the President, and read with him the papers of which exact copies were furnished to the Richmond journals for publication. I am, therefore, able to vouch personally for the fact that the passage as to the killing of the President and Cabinet existed in the original, and the photographic copy leaves no room for doubt upon the point."[5]

Accompanying the letter was a copy of a proclamation by Jefferson Davis setting April 8 as a day of humiliation, fasting, and prayer in accordance with a resolution of the Confederate Congress. The Secretary of State pointed out that in his proclamation the President noted that "a nefarious scheme to burn and plunder our capital, and to destroy our civil government by putting to death the chosen servants of the people, has been baffled and set at naught."[6]

It was the 28th before Benjamin was able to mail the photographic copies. "They speak for themselves, and require no comment," he wrote Slidell. "You will agree with me that they should be extensively circulated, as the most conclusive evidence of the nature of the war now waged against us by those who profess to desire that we should live with them as brethren under one Government." [7]

In the meantime Admiral Dahlgren, who had arrived in Washington from Charleston harbor on the day his son was ambushed, was trying frantically to have Ulric's body removed to friendly soil. He made several trips to Fortress Monroe—four by the 29th of March—pleading frantically with Butler, who in turn pressed the matter with Judge Ould, the Confederate Commissioner of Exchange. After a few days Butler reported to Secretary of War Stanton: "We have not received Colonel Dahlgren's body, for reasons which I believe are not within the control of the Confederate officers." [8] A little later he wrote Dahlgren: "I have received the most positive assurances from Judge Ould upon two points that may interest you. First, that the statements in the Richmond papers of any indignities to the remains of your son are false; that they were decently and properly buried under the direction of an officer of equal rank in the Confederate service. Secondly, I have the most positive assurances from him that you shall receive the remains of your son by next flag-of-truce boat." [9]

By the end of March the Confederates were prepared to file formal protest concerning the Dahlgren papers. At the direction of Jefferson Davis, the originals and four sets of photographic copies were forwarded to General Lee. A covering letter explained: "The Government is in possession of ample and incontestable evidence that the papers were taken from the body, which was identified as that of Colonel Dahlgren." Attention was called to the passages directing that Richmond be burned and Davis and Cabinet killed. Lee was told to open correspondence with Meade to ascertain whether the orders and instructions contained in the papers conformed to those of the young colonel's government or superior officers, and whether "the Government of the United States sanctions the sentiments and purposes therein set forth." [10] As for the

originals of the papers, Lee was told he might retain them as
long as he considered necessary, after which he was to return
them to the Adjutant General's Office.[11]

The day after the papers went out from headquarters,
Fitzhugh Lee forwarded to the Adjutant General's Office the
notebook retained by Colonel Beale at the time Pollard was on
his way to Richmond. With it went a brief explanation, as
well as the following assurance: "His name and rank is written on the first page, with the date (probably) of his purchas-
ing it. The book, amongst other memoranda, contains a rough
pencil sketch of his address to his troops, differing somewhat
from his pen-and-ink copy. I embrace this occasion to add,
the original papers bore no marks of alteration, nor could they
have possibly been changed except by the courier who
brought them to me, which is in the highest degree improb-
able, and the publication of them in the Richmond papers
were exact copies in every respect of the originals." [12]

As directed, General Lee wrote Meade. His letter was prepared on April 1 and sent to Jeb Stuart to be forwarded, but
there was some delay before it could be delivered. Rains had
swollen the streams and it was impossible to cross the Robert-
son River at the point where flags of truce were received by
the Federal commanders. But by the 16th Lee's letter had
reached its destination, for on that date Meade redirected it to
Washington. That same day Meade ordered Kilpatrick to
come to headquarters and to forward a copy of his letter of
March 16, in which he reported the result of his questioning
of the officers and men who accompanied Dahlgren. Instead
of forwarding his letter of March 16, Kilpatrick apparently
wrote a new letter, much of it an exact duplicate of the earlier
missive, but concluding: "The photographic papers referred
to are true copies of the papers approved by me, save so far as
they speak of 'exhorting the prisoners to destroy and burn
the hateful city and kill the traitor Davis and his Cabinet,' and
in this, that they do not contain the indorsement referred to

as having been placed by me on Colonel Dahlgren's papers. Colonel Dahlgren received no orders from me to pillage, burn, or kill, nor were any such instructions given me by my superiors." [13]

In his letter Lee, after setting forth the most incendiary passages from the Dahlgren papers, asked simply whether the Federal government had authorized or sanctioned them. Meade replied that "neither the United States Government, myself, nor General Kilpatrick authorized, sanctioned, or approved the burning of the city of Richmond and the killing of Mr. Davis and Cabinet, nor any other act not required by military necessity and in accordance with the usages of war." In confirmation of this assurance he enclosed a copy of Kilpatrick's letter of April 16.

But Meade's reply was dictated by his official capacity as commander of the Army of the Potomac and not by his personal convictions in the matter. The day after wording his letter to Lee he wrote Mrs. Meade of his correspondence with the Confederate general. "This was a pretty ugly piece of business," he confided, "for in denying having authorized or approved 'the burning of Richmond, or killing Mr. Davis and Cabinet,' I necessarily threw odium on Dahlgren. I, however, enclosed a letter from Kilpatrick, in which the authenticity of the papers was impugned; but I regret to say Kilpatrick's reputation, and collateral evidence in my possession, rather go against this theory. However, I was determined my skirts should be clear, so I promptly disavowed having ever authorized, sanctioned or approved of any act not required by military necessity, and in accordance with the usages of war." [14]

At Army of the Potomac headquarters Provost Marshal General Marsena Patrick, who had written in his diary regarding Kilpatrick's expedition that "I am afraid he will accomplish nothing," shared Meade's feelings and had something to put in writing concerning the papers. Captain John McEntee, among surviving officers who had taken part in the

raid, came into Patrick's quarters one morning when the
provost marshal was going about his business in the usual way,
and the two of them had quite a conversation. That night
Patrick wrote in his diary of McEntee's visit: "He has the
same opinion of Kilpatrick that I have, and says he managed
just as all cowards do. He further says that he thinks the
papers are correct that were found upon Dahlgren, as they
correspond with what D. [Dahlgren] told him. . . ." [15]

Notwithstanding the opinions of certain Northern officers,
a thoroughly agitated public in the North was preparing a
case against the Confederate States government—a set of
charges intended to clear the name of the blond-haired colonel
who had given a leg and then his life for the Union and who
was now disintegrating in some unmarked grave. And therein
lay a mystery.

Spurred by Admiral Dahlgren, Butler relayed through official channels a request for the return of the body. So Judge
Ould rode out to the tent of Lieutenant Colonel Atkinson,
the officer who had superintended the burial, and asked to be
shown the grave, explaining that he wished to have the remains disinterred so they could be taken down on the next
exchange boat for delivery to the father. But Atkinson refused: he had been directed by Jefferson Davis to divulge the
burial site to no one.[16]

A few days later, however, a sergeant brought a note to Atkinson. In it President Davis directed the officer to point out
the grave, explaining that return of the body would be of material advantage to the Confederacy.[17] Atkinson accordingly
ordered his horse and conducted the sergeant to Oakwood
Cemetery, where he indicated the place of burial. It was near
the entrance, unmarked except for a young sapling planted
on its crest.

As they rode away, Atkinson thought he had forever disposed of his responsibility in the burial of Dahlgren. But such
was not the case. A few days later he received a sharp re-

proach from the President: the grave had been opened and found empty, so Davis assumed the officer had disobeyed orders and confided in someone before he received the note brought by the sergeant. But this Atkinson emphatically denied, leaving it the turn of Confederate authorities to be mystified.

Who had exhumed Dahlgren's body and where was it now? Frantic efforts were made to find an answer, but not the slightest trail had been left by the grave-robbers. Whoever they were, after removing the body, they had replaced the dirt, heaped it up, and replanted the young sapling just where it was when the burial detail directed by Atkinson had completed its chores.

Baffled, Ould finally reported to Butler, who passed the word along to Admiral Dahlgren: the grave, when opened, was empty, and "the most vigorous and persistent search" failed to locate the body.

But a few days later Butler had more to report: "I have reliable information from Richmond that Colonel Dahlgren's body has been taken possession of by his Union friends, and has been put beyond the reach of the Rebel authorities." Next day he was able to send the admiral another message:

"The remains are not so far within my control as to be able to remove them from Richmond, where every effort is being made by the detectives to find them; but they are, I am informed and believe, in the hands of devoted friends of the Union, who have taken possession of them in order that proper respect may be shown to them at a time which I trust is not far distant. I hardly dare suggest to Ould, when he reports to me, as he will, that he cannot find them, that I can put them into his possession, because that will show such a correspondence with Richmond as will alarm them, and will redouble their vigilance to detect my sources of information. I am, however, under the direction of the President." [18]

This latest information was not exactly a surprise to the

admiral. A few days earlier a stranger had gained an interview on the claim of having news of Ulric. The stranger whispered that he had been sent by Union friends in Richmond to give assurance that the remains were in good hands and eventually would be returned to Washington.

Meanwhile in Richmond the mystery continued—more puzzling than ever, if anything—for the "Union friends" who could give the answers were few, and they were capable of keeping a secret. It would be years before the full story was known, and then it was too late to matter.

At the time of the search for Dahlgren's body, residents of Richmond apparently gave little attention to the activities of one F. W. E. Lohman, grocer, doing business down in the ghetto area of the city. Some folks were suspicious about his allegiance to the South, but they had no evidence on which to convict. Lohman depended upon Southerners for his business, and he was too smart to talk to the wrong people.

One of the loafers who came to while away the time around the hot stove in Lohman's store was Martin Meredith Lipscomb, a gem of a local character who seemed to feel he was placed on earth for a special purpose and who talked like a member of King Arthur's Round Table. His conversation, spiced with such advice as, "Strike high, even if you lose your hatchet," could liven up even the life of a besieged city; and it had become especially interesting since Lipscomb supervised the burial of the Yankee dead in Oakwood Cemetery.

Lohman frequently stood by when Martin Meredith Lipscomb expounded, and there was design in the grocer's friendly attentiveness. He had a hunch that Dahlgren's body lay somewhere out there among the scattered mounds of Oakwood and that this loquacious ghoul could help him find it.

Having gradually worked into Lipscomb's confidence, one day, when they sat alone, Lohman asked questions of his guest. Had Martin helped bury Dahlgren? No. Could he find out—for a distinguished American admiral, the father of this dead soldier boy, a great and friendly man who was working for the good of the Union, striving to bring the torn sections back together and wield them into a greater nation? Maybe. Then would he be a patriot and assist Friend Lohman of whose hospitality he, Martin Meredith Lipscomb, so frequently partook? Of course.

So Lipscomb went forth, moved now by the purpose of disinterring a body rather than burying one. His snooping was confined to the Negro workmen at Oakwood, for among them he suspected he would find the answer. As he asked his questions, one of the attendants seemed more nervous and excitable than the others, and on him the trail centered. The Negro squirmed. This white man who was pressing for information was the boss; he it was who directed the burial details, who told a worker when to handle his shovel and where to drive his pick, and his word was the law. The Negro finally talked. Yassuh, he knew where Dahlgren was buried. He was on duty the day Colonel Atkinson had arrived with the street wagon bearing a coffin, and he had been chased along with the other laborers into another part of the cemetery until this box could be disposed of. But he had peeped. He had stolen back to the edge of the trees, had watched the proceedings, and he could point out the very grave.

Lipscomb brought Lohman to the cemetery. There they conferred with the Negro, but he closed up tighter than a clam, too frightened to talk in front of an outsider. And he had his reasons: the white folks got angry easily these days, and during a war death was so cheap a man was making a mistake not to mind his own business. The boss passed over some crinkly Confederate currency, an effective persuader when mixed with the right words, and the workman walked away to toss a rock on the mound in question while his audience stood at a discreet distance.

At nine o'clock on the night of April 6 Lipscomb and Lohman and the latter's brother, John, got into a wagon in the heart of the city and rode eastward toward Oakwood. The weather was clear; a rain, following on the heels of several inches of snow, had stopped at noon, and now the wind was to the northwest and cool. At ten o'clock, in darkness ideal for their purpose, the mysterious trio drew up at the cemetery. Waiting for them was the workman who had tossed the stone, and with him were two of his companions.

Soon from the black shadows came the thud of the pick, the scrape of the shovel, the hefty grunt of laborers applying their muscle. Winds of early April soughed through the trees, lonely lullabies in a yard of skeletons and corpses and tombstones. The dark-skinned trio dug while their white brethren waited at the gate, prepared to assume innocence if discovered by some casual night-walker. These men at the gate had chores too. The mule hitched to the wagon, sniffing the tainted air arising from shallow graves, attempted again and again to break away, and it took all their might to hold him back.

Twenty minutes after the Negroes started digging they appeared out of the dark bearing a coffin. Lohman directed that it be placed on the ground and opened, and as the lid was raised he ran his hand inside. Satisfied the delivery was correct, he handed over $1500 in Confederate notes, a reasonable sum even in inflated currency, and reminded them that, to complete the job, the grave must be refilled and the seedling replanted.

More than an hour later the three white men rolled into the flicker of the gaslights of Church Hill. Their goal was the home of William S. Rowlett, a Union sympathizer living on Chelsea Hill, a half-mile to the northeast. Down Broad Street to Seventeenth, along Seventeenth to its northern terminus, and thence up the hill to Rowlett's they drove, cursing their balky mule at regular intervals. It was two o'clock in the morning when they drew rein.

Carefully next morning, a bright spring day, the word was

spread, and one by one Union friends came, among them Betty Van Lew. They stared at the body of their dead hero, laid out in the privacy of a seed house at the Rowlett home. It was Betty who wrote an account of what they saw and did:

"Colonel Dahlgren's hair was very short, but all that could be spared was cut off and sent to his father before Richmond fell. Gentle hands and tearful eyes examined the breast to see if there was any around there, but nothing of the kind could be perceived. The body, except the head, was in a perfect state of preservation, fair, pure and firm the flesh, here and there a purple spot as of mildew. This was remarkable considering the length of time of the burial, unless, as was thought, it was becoming adipocere, the ground in which he was buried being very damp. The comeliness of the young face was gone, yet the features seemed regular, and there was a wonderful look of firmness or energy stamped upon them. His dress was a shirt of the coarsest kind, not even fastened; pantaloons of dark blue cloth; a fine cotton sock was on his left foot, the right leg was wanting below the knee, his right hand was carelessly thrown across his person, the left, robbed of its little finger, was resting on his left thigh." [19]

During the morning a metallic casket was brought from the city, and the body, wrapped in a blue military blanket, placed in it. Around noon a wagon loaded with young fruit trees, so thickly packed into the vehicle as to hide the huge box beneath them, was driven away from the farm by Rowlett.[20] It was on its way through outer Richmond lines to another temporary grave, this one on the farm of Robert Orrick, a German living in the vicinity of Hungary Station on the R. F. & P. Railroad.

Rowlett was not without a narrow escape en route. He rolled up to the picket's tent just as another wagon going in the opposite direction was searched. Pulling in his horse, he dropped the reins and took on an attitude of ease while the guard finished searching the other vehicle.

"Whose fruit trees are these?" asked the picket when he approached. And then, without waiting for an answer: "I think I have seen your face before."

"Yes, and I have yours," said Rowlett.

"Where?"

"At the house where you stay."

"But whose trees are these?"

"They belong to a German out here in the country. I'm hauling them to him."

"Isn't it kind of late to transplant them?"

Just then, before the question could be answered, another vehicle passing in the opposite direction rolled up, and the guard looked it over hastily before returning to his conversation with Rowlett.

"You say it's not too late to transplant them?"

"I hope not."

"Well, you've got them packed in there so nicely I hate to disturb them."

"When I packed them," said Rowlett, "I did not expect them to be disturbed, but as it is, being a citizen, I know a soldier's duty and expect him to do it, so of course you must take them out."

But the guard waved him on. "I won't keep you any longer. I think it's all right, at any rate. Your honest face is guarantee enough for me. Go on." [21]

In the late afternoon, at the Orrick farm, the metallic casket was lifted from its hiding place beneath the peach seedlings. A shallow grave in an open field awaited it, and there it was deposited as the sun was sinking. Dirt was thrown in upon it and shaped into a low, circular mound, on which was planted one of the young fruit trees, a seal to hide a secret until the end of the war.

14

Memoranda of Guilt

THE CONTROVERSY OVER the Dahlgren papers raged on. The Federals were denying everything and accusing the South of having planted the documents on the raider's body to make the North appear a ruthless aggressor in the eyes of the nations abroad. What was worse, even men of integrity siding with the Union refused to weigh the facts in the case and to accept what the Confederate government looked upon as obvious and indisputable. When Mrs. Jefferson Davis mentioned this to one prominent visitor of Federal sympathies, he asked, "Did you believe it?" This brought instant reaction from the lady. She said there had been no time for a forgery and that, besides, an itinerary written in the same hand had been found in the notebook. Her guest made some laughing remark of disbelief, whereupon she offered to have it brought for his examination. But at this suggestion he merely hunched his shoulders and laughed again, remarking, "Now, the fact is I do not want to believe it, and if you could convince me I would rather not look at it."

Mrs. Davis could sympathize with this attitude. "I had felt

much the same unwillingness, having been intimate with the parents," she explained afterward. "Once Commodore Dahlgren had brought the little fair-haired boy to show me how pretty he looked in his black velvet suit and Vandyke collar, and I could not reconcile the two Ulrics." [1]

As far as the Southern people were concerned, this notebook Mrs. Davis offered to show her guest was the clincher in the evidence pointing to the authenticity of the papers. Writing of it in her diary, Mrs. Chesnut said: "Now that Dahlgren has failed to carry out his orders, the Yankees disown them; they disavow it all. He was not sent here to murder us all, hang the President, and burn the town. There is the notebook, however, at the Executive Office, with the orders to hang and burn." [2]

The *Examiner*, too, felt that the memorandum book was the deciding factor in the argument. "We are permitted," stated its editor, "to copy these private memoranda, which confirm Dahlgren's guilt beyond a doubt and add to his crimes even a blacker shade than has yet been given them. It should be a convincing reply to the Northern denial of the authenticity of the Dahlgren documents heretofore published." The *Examiner* further reported that, besides presenting the notebook to the War Department, Fitzhugh Lee had written a letter explaining that there was no opportunity to alter the papers found with it, unless it were done by the courier to whom they were entrusted, and that he himself could positively state that no writing whatever had been interlined in them.

At the War Department the notebook fell under the eyes of General Gorgas, the Confederacy's efficient ordnance chief, and that night he made an entry in his diary: "I saw today in the hands of General F. H. Lee the pocket memo book of Dahlgren, in which is a rough draft in pencil of his published address to his troops, differing a little here and there;

and among other memoranda on another page: 'Jeff Davis and his Cabinet must be killed on the spot.' " [3]

Halbach, who next to William Littlepage was closest to the origin of the papers, gave the following explanation of the "utter absurdity and falsehood" of the Northern charge that they were forgeries:

"1. The papers were taken by Littlepage from the person of a man whose name he had never heard. It was a dark night, and the captor, with the aid of the noon-day sun, could not write at all. I afterwards taught him to write a little in my school. The question occurs: Can a boy who cannot write at all write such papers, and sign to them an unknown name? If they had been forged by anyone else, would they have been placed in the hands of a child? Could anyone else have forged an unknown and unheard of name?

"2. The papers were handed to me immediately after their capture, in the presence of gentlemen of undoubted veracity and integrity, before whom I can prove that the papers not only were not, but could not have been, altered or interpolated by myself. These gentlemen were with me every moment of the time between my receiving the papers and delivering them to Lieutenant Pollard.

"3. If Lieutenant Pollard had made any alterations in the papers, these would have been detected by everyone who read the papers before they were given to him, and afterwards read them in the newspapers. But all agree that they were correctly copied. In short, human testimony cannot establish any fact more fully than the fact that Colonel Ulrich Dahlgren was the author of the 'Dahlgren Papers.' " [4]

Among those who saw the papers while they were still in Halbach's hands next morning was the Baptist minister, the Reverend Richard Hugh Bagby. He later stated emphatically that the copies in the Richmond papers were identical with the originals. So testified Lieutenant Pollard, Colonel Beale, General Fitzhugh Lee, and Heros von Borcke, the only other men through whose hands they passed before delivery to Jefferson Davis. Lee gave it as his opinion that the memoranda and address found on Dahlgren's body were based upon the general instructions to Kilpatrick's entire command.[5] Von Borcke's statement was addressed to the editor of the London *Times* and was published in the fall of 1869.[6]

The North could think of two reasons why the Confederate government would want to plant the papers on Dahlgren's body: first, to inflame the Southerners to greater effort both at home and on the battlefield and, second, to persuade the British and French to come to the aid of the South. But the strongest evidence of forgery cited was the fact that the name signed to the address was somehow or other spelled "Dalhgren" instead of "Dahlgren," and that it was accompanied only by the initial "U," whereas the deceased had usually spelled out the first name in his signature. In his memoir of the son, Admiral Dahlgren concluded that the misspelling was all the evidence needed to prove the papers a fake.

But this was evading the issue. The statement in the papers that incensed the South most was the reference to burning Richmond and killing Jefferson Davis and Cabinet. It appeared most emphatically in the set of instructions, more so than on the paper with the incorrect signature. And again, it was in Dahlgren's memorandum book, accompanied by the additional words "on the spot."

These instructions obviously were for Captain Mitchell, the officer who had been detached by Dahlgren to conduct the ambulances and led horses down the north bank of the James. They told in detail the course he was to follow, the destruction he was to wreak en route, and what was to be done after reaching Richmond. This, more importantly than anything else, seems to point to the genuineness of the papers. It would have been clairvoyance for the South to have known that Dahlgren's column was to be divided, and it would have been the finest bit of fiction on record for someone on the Rebel side to have originated in detail Mitchell's course of action.

In denying the authenticity of the papers, Federal authorities confined their reference to the address, the wording of which was not nearly so objectionable, after all, as that of the set of instructions and the memorandum book. They denied emphatically that the address was ever delivered to Dahlgren's column, but no one testified that Mitchell had not received his orders. Mitchell himself revealed the orders were given him on the morning of March 1 near the Horton home, as they approached the James, and said about the papers only: "I would state that no address of any kind was ever published to either officers or men."[7] The inquiry directed by Meade referred only to the address. Kilpatrick, in his reply, confined his remarks to the same subject. Subsequently, in his report of April 16, he did allude to "the instructions," but treated them in a blanket denial. But the cavalry leader's assertion was discounted even by Meade, who wrote his wife that "Kilpatrick's reputation," as well as collateral evidence in his possession, went against the theory that the papers were faked. Supporting this attitude was Marsena Patrick's record regarding what Dahlgren had told Captain McEntee before starting the raid. Another condemning factor, as Judah Benjamin pointed out in his message to Slidell, was the indulgence of Northern newspapers "in their usual boasts in the intended sack" of Richmond.

Historians and others even to the present generation have toyed with the idea that the papers were planted.[8] And there are unanswered questions that make the subject a rich field for speculation, with convictions varying by locality. Was the handwriting on the papers and in the notebook Dahlgren's? Mrs. Jefferson Davis, who indicated she examined them, said the handwriting on the papers and that in the notebook were identical.[9] Disappearance of all evidence except one of the photographic copies of the address, now on file at the United

States Department of Archives and faint almost to the point of illegibility, makes this difficult to answer today. If Kilpatrick approved the address in red ink just before the raid began, what happened to the copy so marked? No trace of this, either in record or hearsay, has been found.

While the war was still in progress, the opposing sections of the country debated, and Dahlgren became a name of infamy in the South. In the North his friends and relatives waited patiently to pay their last respects to his remains and their tribute to the adventure that had brought about his disrepute below the Potomac.

The war ended. Then one day the following fall Dahlgren's remains, exhumed from the temporary grave near Richmond and encased in a casket more fitting his station in life, came into Washington. There it lay in state for hours in the council chamber of the city. Next day, after full military honors and an eloquent eulogy by that controversial Congregational minister, Henry Ward Beecher, it was taken by train to Philadelphia, to lie in time-honored Independence Hall. Around it gathered the mayor and other dignitaries, each paying tribute by his presence, and the Reverend Doctor J. P. Wilson, who had baptized Ulric as a boy, uttered the final oration. Then the funeral cortege moved to Laurel Hill Cemetery. Mourners at the graveside included General Meade and his chief of staff, A. A. Humphreys. It was November 1, 1865.

Noticeably absent from these final obsequies was Kilpatrick, the man most intimately concerned with the untimely end of the young soldier. Twice the two had been together in action—at Boonsboro, where Dahlgren lost a leg, and on the raid to Richmond, where he lost his life. And at the moment it would seem that the general had no logical excuse for his failure of attendance: after months of fighting with Sherman's army, he was on leave of absence awaiting orders.

Sixteen more years of life, zestful and active life, were ahead for Kilpatrick. He continued his career as a rake with women of low virtue of all colors, and the day came when he led his riotous horsemen through the deep South, waving to them from an open vehicle in which he cavorted with a prostitute. By 1866 he was out of the service, ready to devote his energies to other pursuits. He stumped the country as a lecturer. He edited a magazine for ladies. He became a gentleman farmer, with liveried butler and fine vintages. He hunted wild pigs in the woods. And he ran unsuccessfully for the governorship of New Jersey, thus failing to realize the ambition that had steered some of his courses during the war. He wound up as United States Minister to Chile, married a native woman, became president of a fashionable club in Santiago, and died before he was forty-six. The Chilean government honored him with a public funeral.

Long years afterward Kilpatrick received a kind of recognition he would have much preferred. *Allatoona*, the melodrama he had written during his theatrical phase, was dusted off, given a new name—*The Blue and the Gray, or War Is Hell*—and presented in the old Rialto Theater in Hoboken.[10] It ran for fifty-two performances.

Whatever Judson Kilpatrick might be accused of, it could never be said that he was opposed to variety.

APPENDIX

The Dahlgren Papers

The address to his command:

Headquarters Third Division Cavalry Corps

————————————, 186—.

Officers and Men:

You have been selected from brigades and regiments as a picked command to attempt a desperate undertaking—an undertaking which, if successful, will write your names on the hearts of your countrymen in letters that can never be erased, and which will cause the prayers of our fellow-soldiers now confined in loathsome prisons to follow you and yours wherever you may go. We hope to release the prisoners from Belle Island first, and having seen them fairly started, we will cross the James River into Richmond, destroying the bridges after us and exhorting the released prisoners to destroy and burn the hateful city; and do not allow the Rebel leader Davis and his traitorous crew to escape. The prisoners must render great assistance, as you cannot leave your ranks too far or become too much scattered, or you will be lost. Do not allow any personal gain to lead you off, which would only bring you to an ignominious death at the hands of citizens. Keep well together and obey orders strictly and all will be well; but on no account scatter too far, for in union there is strength. With strict obedience to orders and fearlessness in the execution you will be sure to succeed. We will join the main force on the other side of the city, or perhaps meet them inside. Many of you may fail; but if there is any man here not willing to sacrifice his life in such a great and glorious undertaking, or who does not feel capable of meeting the enemy in such a desperate fight as will follow, let him step out, and he may go hence to the arms of his sweetheart and read of the braves who swept through the city of Richmond. We want no man who cannot feel sure of success in such a holy cause. We will have a desperate fight, but stand up to it when it comes and all will be well. Ask the blessing of the Almighty and do not fear the enemy.

U. DALHGREN,
COLONEL, COMMANDING.

Dahlgren's instructions to Captain John F. B. Mitchell of the Second New York Cavalry for leading a separate detachment down the north bank of the James, keeping pace with the main force under the young colonel that was to cross and proceed along the south bank:

Guides.—Pioneers (with oakum, turpentine, and torpedoes), signal officer, quartermaster, commissary. Scouts and pickets. Men in Rebel uniform. These will remain on the north bank and move down with the force on the south bank, not getting ahead of them, and if the communication can be kept up without giving an alarm it must be done; but everything depends upon a surprise, and no one must be allowed to pass ahead of the column. Information must be gathered in regard to the crossings of the river, so that should we be repulsed on the south side we will know where to recross at the nearest point. All mills must be burned and the canal destroyed, and also everything which can be used by the Rebels must be destroyed, including the boats on the river. Should a ferry-boat be seized and can be worked, have it moved down. Keep the force on the south side posted of any important movement of the enemy, and in case of danger some of the scouts must swim the river and bring us information. As we approach the city the party must take great care that they do not get ahead of the other party on the south side, and must conceal themselves and watch our movements. We will try and secure the bridge to the city, one mile below Belle Isle, and release the prisoners at the same time. If we do not succeed they must then dash down, and we will try and carry the bridge from each side. When necessary, the men must be filed through the woods and along the river bank. The bridges once secured, and the prisoners loose and over the river, the bridges will be burned and the city destroyed. The men must keep together and well in hand, and once in the city it must be destroyed and Jeff. Davis and Cabinet killed. Pioneers will go along with combustible material. The officer must use his discretion about the time of assisting us. Horses and cattle which we do not need immediately must be shot rather than left. Everything on the canal and elsewhere of service to the Rebels must be destroyed. As General Custer may follow me, be careful not to give a false alarm.

General instructions:

The Signal Officer must be prepared to communicate at night by rockets, and in other things pertaining to his department.

The quartermasters and commissaries must be on the lookout for their departments, and see that there are no delays on their account.

The engineer officer will follow to survey the road as we pass over it, etc.

The pioneers must be prepared to construct a bridge or destroy one. They must have plenty of oakum and turpentine for burning, which will be rolled in soaked balls and given to the men to burn when we get in the city. Torpedoes will only be used by the pioneers for destroying the main bridges, etc. They must be prepared to destroy railroads. Men will branch off to the right with a few pioneers and destroy the bridges and railroads south of Richmond, and then join us at the city. They must be well prepared with torpedoes, etc. The line of Falling Creek is probably the best to work along, or as they approach the city Goode's Creek, so that no reinforcements can come up on any cars. No one must be allowed to pass ahead for fear of communicating news. Rejoin the command with all haste, and if cut off cross the river above Richmond and rejoin us. Men will stop at Bellona Arsenal and totally destroy it, and anything else but hospitals; then follow on and rejoin the command at Richmond with all haste, and if cut off cross the river and rejoin us. As General Custer may follow me, be careful not to give a false alarm.

Early itinerary:

Saturday. Leave camp at dark (Six P.M.). Cross Ely's Ford at ten P.M.

Twenty miles—Cross North Anna at four A.M. Sunday—feed and water—one hour.

Three miles—Frederick's Hall Station, six A.M.—destroy art'y, eight A.M.

Twenty miles—Near James river, two P.M. Sunday—feed and water, 1½ hour.

Thirty miles to Richmond—March towards Kilpatrick for one hour, and then, as soon as dark, cross the river, reaching Richmond in the morning (Monday).

One squadron remains on north side, and one squadron to cut the railroad bridge at Falling Creek, and join at Richmond—eighty-three miles.

Gen. K.—cross at one A.M. Sunday—ten miles. Pass river at five A.M. (resistance).

Chilesburg—fourteen miles—eight A.M.

Resistance at North Anna—three miles.

Railroad bridges at South Anna—twenty-six miles—two P.M. Destroy bridges—pass the South Anna and feed until after dark—then signal each other. After dark move down to Richmond, and be in front of the city at daybreak.

Return—in Richmond during the day—feed and water men outside.

Be over the Pamunkey at daybreak—feed and water, and then cross the Rappahannock at night (Tuesday night) when they must be on the lookout.

Spies should be sent on Friday morning early, and be ready to cut.

Notes in memorandum book as they appeared in the Richmond *Examiner* of April 1, 1864:

Pleasonton will govern details.

Will have details from other commands, (four thousand).

Michigan men have started.

Colonel J. H. Devereux has torpedoes.

Hanover Junction (B. T. Johnson). Maryland Line.

Chapin's Farm—Seven miles below Richmond.

One brigade (Hunton's relieved, Wise sent to Charleston).

River can be forded half a mile above the city. No works on south side. Hospitals near them. River fordable. Canal can be crossed.

Fifty men to remain on north bank, and keep in communication if possible. To destroy mills, canal, and burn everything of value to the Rebels. Seize any large ferry boats, and note all crossings, in case we have to return that way. Keep us posted of any important movement of the Rebels, and as we approach the city, communicate with us, and do not give the alarm before they see us in possession of Belle Isle and the bridge. If engaged there or unsuccessful, they must assist in securing the bridges until we cross. If the ferry-boat can be taken and worked, bring it down. Everything that cannot be secured or made use of must be destroyed. Great care must be taken not to be seen or any alarm given. The men must be filed along off the road or along the main bank. When we enter the city the officer must use his discretion as to when to assist in crossing the bridges.

The prisoners once loosed and the bridges crossed, the city must be destroyed, burning the public buildings, etc.

Prisoners to go with party.

Spike the heavy guns outside.

Pioneers must be ready to repair, destroy, etc. Turpentine will be provided. The pioneers must be ready to destroy the Richmond bridges, after we have all crossed, and to destroy the railroad near Frederick's Hall (station, artillery, etc.).

Fifteen men to halt at Bellona Arsenal, while the column goes on, and destroy it. Have some prisoners. Then rejoin us at

Richmond, leaving a portion to watch if anything follows, under a good officer.

Will be notified that Custer may come.

Main column, four hundred.

One hundred men will take the bridge after the scouts, and dash through the streets and open the way to the front, or if it is open destroy everything in the way.

While they are on the big bridges, one hundred men will take Belle Isle, after the scouts, instructing the prisoners to gut the city. The reserve (two hundred) will see this fairly done and everything over, and then follow, destroying the bridges after them, but not scattering too much, and always having a part well in hand.

Jeff. Davis and Cabinet must be killed on the spot.

NOTES

CHAPTER 1

1. For a description of this building see *History of the One Hundred and Sixth Regiment Pennsylvania Volunteers*, by Joseph R. C. Ward (Philadelphia, Grant Faires and Rodgers, 1863), p. 103.
2. *Diary of a Young Officer*, by J. M. Favill (Chicago, R. R. Donnelley & Sons Company, 1909), p. 123.
3. *South After Gettysburg: Letters of Cornelia Hancock from the Army of the Potomac*, edited by Henrietta Stratton Jaquette (New York, Thomas Y. Crowell Company, 1956), p. 53.
4. The mansion at Stevensburg in which Kilpatrick stayed, a fine old home overlooking the village from a grove of trees a short distance south of State Highway Number 3, is now the residence of J. A. Covington. Natives still talk of the general's behavior while there and the gay moment when he, despite all his teetotaling sobriety, rode his horse through the wide center hallway of the building, putting scars on the floors to be observed by future generations.
5. *Civil War Echoes: Character Sketches and State Secrets*, by Hamilton Gay Howard (Washington, Howard Publishing Company, 1907), p. 214.
6. *Personal Recollections of a Cavalryman*, by J. H. Kidd (Ionia, Michigan, Sentinel Printing Company, 1908).
7. This figure was used by General Meade in a letter to his wife. See *The Life and Letters of George Gordon Meade* (New York, Charles Scribner's Sons, 1913), II, 167, referred to hereafter as Meade.
8. This was the expression used by General Meade in writing his wife two days after the ball.

9. *A Woman's War Record*, by Septima M. Collis (New York, G. P. Putnam's Sons, 1889), p. 34.

CHAPTER 2

1. *Official Records of the Rebellion*, Series 2, VI, 279, referred to hereafter as *O.R.*
2. Report of John Wilkins, surgeon of Hospital Number Twenty-one, Richmond, Virginia. (See *ibid.*, p. 1089.)
3. This was charged by Judge Robert Ould, Confederate Agent of Exchange, in a letter to Brigadier General John H. Winder, who had the responsibility of policing Richmond. (See *ibid.*, p. 267.)
4. Report of United States Surgeon Thomas A. McParlin. *Ibid.*, p. 474.
5. *Ibid.*, VIII, 343.
6. This precautionary habit was revealed by Miss Van Lew herself in an inscription in her handwriting on the front of her personal journal. The record, now in the New York Public Library, was long buried for safety and is not in too good condition. Much of it was written on the back of paper bearing the official letterhead, "Office of Provost Marshal General, Armies Operating Against Richmond, Va., Fortress Monroe, Va., 186—." A copy of it was made for the Confederate Museum at Richmond by Mrs. Charles Morrison of that city and now is on file in Metal Case 3-V854a. It was made available to the author through the kindness of Miss India Thomas, regent of the museum, and her assistant, Miss Eleanor Brockenborough.
7. A copy of this circular is on file in records of the Third Division, Cavalry Corps, at the National Archives.
8. Memoirs of Major Abner R. Small in *The Road to Richmond* (Berkeley, California, University of California Press, 1939).
9. *O.R.*, Series 1, XXXIII, 530.
10. Tom Abraham was sentenced to death and executed by firing squad at Yorktown, Virginia, March 7, 1864. For an eyewitness account, see *The Rebellion Record*, edited by Frank Moore (New York, G. P. Putnam, 1863), VIII, 579.

CHAPTER 3

1. The factors that influenced Lincoln in his decision favoring the raid on Richmond are obvious. Libby's prison break occurred February 8. On the 11th, with scarcely time enough intervening for any of the soldiers to have made their way from Richmond to Washington in that day of slow travel, via the roundabout route that would have had to be followed in order to avoid Wade Hampton's troops north of the Confederate capital, he issued the initial order that would get the raid started. The first written communication with him from any of the escapees, as far as this author has been able to ascertain, was dated on the 21st, well after plans for the expedition were fully under way. (See *O.R.*, Series 2, VI, 977.)
2. *Ibid.*, Series 1, XXXIII, 552.
3. *Ibid.*, p. 171.
4. Some students of the war have theorized that General Pleasonton's opinion in this instance, though substantiated by later developments, was the beginning of his fall from grace at Washington. In a short time he was removed from command of the cavalry in the Eastern Theater and ordered to active duty elsewhere.
5. *Ibid.*, p. 170.

CHAPTER 4

1. *South After Gettysburg*, edited by Jaquette, p. 59.
2. This raid, in the opinion of General Sigel, an experienced German soldier, "clearly demonstrated the principal which I have always tried to impress on the minds of our cavalry—that in an attack the sword is mightier than the carbine and pistol." See *Memoir of Ulric Dahlgren*, by Admiral John A. Dahlgren (Philadelphia, J. B. Lippincott and Company, 1872), p. 113, referred to hereafter as Dahlgren. This theory, of course, was completely contrary to that of Confederate Partisan Leader John Singleton Mosby, most famous of the guerrillas of that era, who taught his Rangers that the pistol was much more effective in cavalry action than any other weapon.

3. Hamilton Gay Howard, in *Civil War Echoes*, p. 220, tells of watching Dahlgren as he rode along in a dress parade at Brandy Station the following February and describes him as having "lost his right leg below the knee." The bullet struck Dahlgren in the ankle bone and passed out through the top of his foot. Immediately after he was wounded, he turned to E. A. Paul, correspondent for the New York *Times*, and said: "Paul, I have got it at last." Together, some time later, they rode to a surgeon. (See the New York *Times*, March 9, 1864.)

4. Letters to Mrs. M. M. Dahlgren, now in the Manuscript Division, Library of Congress.

5. *The Diary of Edward Bates*, in *American Historical Association Reports* (Washington, D.C., United States Government Printing Office, 1933), IV, 309.

6. Kilpatrick got off on the wrong foot with the Baltimore & Ohio Railroad early in the war. As his regiment entrained at Baltimore in September, '61, en route to Washington, he apparently became suspicious of the loyalty of the train crew and stationed four men with loaded pistols on the engine and two others back in the train, the former to stand guard over the engineer and the latter over the conductor. This brought formal protest from W. P. Smith, master of transportation, who pointed out that it might have led to "fearful results if any accident or irregularity had occurred to induce the use of the weapons." (See *Records of the Military Railroads*, War Records Section, U. S. Department of Archives.)

7. Kilpatrick was graduated seventeenth in the class of '61 at West Point.

8. Remark made by General W. T. Sherman to General J. H. Wilson, as told in *Under the Old Flag* (New York, D. Appleton and Company, 1912), p. 372.

9. *Meade's Headquarters, 1863-1865*, edited by George R. Agassiz (Boston, The Atlantic Monthly Press, 1922), p. 76.

10. In a farewell address to his old command at the time of his transfer to the West in the spring of '64, Kilpatrick said that the nickname "Kilcavalry" had been unjustly pinned on him. See *Seventh Regiment, Michigan Volunteer Cavalry*, by Asa B. Isham (New York, Town Topics Publishing Company, 1893), p. 40.

11. This account is given by Captain H. C. Parson, 1st Vermont Cavalry, an eyewitness, in *The Blue and the Gray*, edited by Professor J. Warren Gilbert (Harrisburg, Pennsylvania, Evangelical Press, 1922), p. 144.

12. For a modern-day evaluation of Kilpatrick, the author asked the opinion of that distinguished war hero and military student, Brigadier General Carl A. Beahr, veteran artillerist who during World War II led American artillery troops through Africa and Italy, and who commanded the VI Corps artillery in the landing in southern France, the advance up Rhone Valley and through the Vosges Mountains, the penetration of the Siegfried Line, the Rhine crossing, and the offensive to Brenner Pass, where the Nineteenth German Army surrendered. This was his description of the Union cavalryman: "Kilpatrick was a mixture of uncalculated recklessness and caution. A dashing leader up to a certain point, he was suddenly apt to become prudent and deficient in resourcefulness, and to rush out of danger as he had into it."

13. Colonel Theodore Lyman to his wife. This letter is reproduced in *Meade's Headquarters, 1863-1865*, p. 76.

14. *O.R.*, Series 1, XXIX, II, 832.

15. Chief of Staff A. A. Humphreys to Brigadier General H. J. Hunt, chief of artillery, *ibid.*, XXXIII, 595.

16. *Ibid.*, p. 173.

17. Pleasonton to Kilpatrick, *ibid.*, p. 183. Dahlgren first had visited Richmond as a sixteen-year-old boy en route to a surveying job along the Mississippi. See Dahlgren, p. 20. Except for that experience, his knowledge would appear to apply largely to the area, especially around Fredericksburg, through which Kilpatrick would have to ride. Some reports, largely unconfirmed and not accompanied by entirely accurate detail, hinted that he had gone to Richmond as a spy early in '63 under the guise of a disaffected Union deserter fleeing in protest of Lincoln's Emancipation Proclamation. See article by Thad Walker in *Blue and Gray*, edited by J. W. Morton, Jr. (Philadelphia, Patriotic Publishing Company, 1893), III, 330.

18. *O.R.*, Series 1, XXXIII, 174.

19. *Ibid.*, p. 606.

20. Letters between Ulric and his father, 1859-1864, in the Manuscript Division, Library of Congress. Italics in this instance are Ulric Dahlgren's.

21. Meade, II, 167.

                         CHAPTER 5

1. Remains of the fireplaces built by the soldiers are still visible in the woods around Stevensburg and at other points up and down the Rappahannock and Rapidan Rivers.

2. Now called Mount Pony by local residents.

3. *Seventh Michigan Volunteer Cavalry*, compiled by William O. Lee (Detroit, Ralston-Stroup Printing Company, 1893), p. 197.

4. *Kilpatrick's Richmond Raid*, by W. H. Spera, in *History of the Seventeenth Regiment Pennsylvania Volunteer Cavalry* (Lebanon, Pennsylvania, Sowers Printing Company, 1911), p. 197, referred to hereafter as Spera.

5. *Personal Reminiscences of Samuel Harris*, published in Spera, p. 70.

6. *O.R.*, Series 1, XXXIII, 609.

7. Some records of the raid say five days' rations were issued, but the most official of these indicate that the issue was for three days.

8. Spera, p. 223.

9. *Ibid.*

10. *O.R.*, Series 1, XXXIII, 175.

11. In his official report of the raid, dated March 16, 1864, Kilpatrick gave the strength of Dahlgren's column as 460. But others, including Captain John F. B. Mitchell, Dahlgren's next in command, and even Kilpatrick in an earlier report, fixed the total at 500. However, the figure used in the latter instance may have resulted from a tendency to employ round numbers. (See *O.R.*, Series 1, XXXIII, 183, 194, 197.)

12. Witnesses disagree as to the hour of Dahlgren's departure, some fixing it as late as 7:00 P.M. But those closest to the action, including Captain Mitchell of the Second New York Cavalry, second in command, gave it as 6:00 P.M.

13. The exact hour of Kilpatrick's departure also has been confused. It is given in official reports and by subsequent writers at periods ranging from 3:00 A.M. to 10:00 P.M. But 7:00 P.M. is most generally accepted and appears to be borne out by reported times of arrival at various points along the route.

The regiments from which this column were selected were the Third Indiana; First Maine; Fifth, Sixth, and Seventh Michigan; Second, Fourth, Fifth, and Sixth New York; Fourth, Seventh, Sixteenth, Seventeenth, and Eighteenth Pennsylvania; and First Vermont. The artillery was taken from Ransom's Regular Battery.

CHAPTER 6

1. *Reports of the United States Military Telegraph,* Office of the Adjutant General, National Archives, Record Group 94, Box 70.

2. Captain Joseph Gloskoski, Twenty-ninth New York Infantry, acting signal officer, in *O.R.,* Series 1, XXXIII, 189.

3. Kilpatrick's combined strength is another point of confusion. In a report from Yorktown on March 6, 1864 (*ibid.,* p. 182), he gave the total as 3858, but ten days later, back at headquarters, he listed it as 3582 (*ibid.,* p. 183). However, an inspector general's report, prepared at Meade's direction, fixed the aggregate at 3595 (*ibid.,* p. 187). This report is on file at the National Archives, Record Group 94, Box 64.

4. Confederate pickets at this time had been considerably thinned by the withdrawal of cavalry for recruiting and supply purposes (*O.R.,* Series 4, III, 324). Ely's Ford was the headquarters of the entire Rebel line from United States Ford up to Germanna Ford. So quietly was the picket post at Ely's wiped out that commanding officers were not sure whether the men on duty had been killed or captured. The captain in charge there was W. B. Young of Cobb's Legion, a crack cavalry outfit. He was considered the best picket officer in his brigade by its commander, who reported: ". . . If I had been called upon for the most reliable officer in my command for any duty I should have selected this captain. To the treachery

of some citizen, whose name I cannot learn, we are indebted for this move." (See *ibid.*, Series 1, XXXIII, 203.)

5. Martin Hogan was breveted several times, first as a lieutenant for recapturing a flag in '61 and last as a major while a prisoner of war. One of the most active soldiers in the Union army, he had arrived in this country from Ireland not quite three years before the outbreak of hostilities. He joined the First Indiana Cavalry at Terre Haute on May 9, 1861, and first saw action in the West Virginia campaign. The following year he was made captain of independent scouts and continued in this service to the end of the war.

Records at the National Archives show that Hogan was captured on April 6, 1864. This would mean that he was taken prisoner after his return from the Kilpatrick raid. However, in a letter to a friend in 1867, while serving with the Thirteenth U. S. Infantry in Montana Territory, he mentions that he was pinned beneath his horse and captured in the third assault on the Richmond fortifications. To add more confusion, some of the Confederates involved in the raid indicate very clearly that Hogan was among prisoners captured from Dahlgren's column at the time of the leader's death.

Hogan was confined for a time at Andersonville Prison, later testifying as a witness in the trial of Henry Wirz, condemned and executed after the war for mistreatment of Federal prisoners while serving as superintendent of the Andersonville Prison. He left the army after fighting the Indians in Montana for several years, and was slain in 1879, while assisting a peace officer, at Maysville, Missouri, where he is buried.

In the *Official Records*, he several times is referred to as "Hogan the Scout." In some of these instances, the indexer, apparently unaware of his true identification, gave him the name of Christopher. The author is indebted to the veteran's grandson, Mort J. Donoghue, 555 Post Street, San Francisco, California, for his help in establishing Christopher and Martin E. as the same man, as well as for supplying additional information concerning his ancestor.

6. *The Rebellion Record*, VIII, 571, Document 134.

7. The guide is identified in a paper read on March 9, 1906, before R. E. Lee Camp, No. 1, Confederate Veterans, by one of its members, Dr. Richard G. Crouch, who lived for a number of years in the vicinity of Contention. He also is mentioned in *Fifth New York Cavalry*, by the Reverend Louis N. Beaudrye (Albany, New York, J. Munsell, 1868), p. 99.

   The author was informed by Harry W. Baldwin, clerk of the Goochland County Circuit Court, that no village by the name of Contention now exists in the area, although the name is applied to the farm of Robert Sherman near Lee Station on the Chesapeake & Ohio Railroad. He knew of no community in adjoining Powhatan County by the name of Centre Hill.

8. *O.R.*, Series 1, XXXIII, 221.

9. *Butler and His Cavalry in the War of Secession, 1861-1865* (Columbia, South Carolina, The State Company, 1909), p. 102.

10. Spera, p. 232.

11. Baltimore *Sun*, March 5, 1864.

12. *The Rebellion Record*, VIII, 573, Document 134.

13. Spera, p. 234.

14. *The Rebellion Record*, VIII, 574.

15. Dahlgren, p. 212.

16. Federal records identify this point at which the paths of the two columns diverged as Mount Pleasant.

17. Spera, p. 235.

18. *O.R.*, Series 1, XXXIII, 615.

19. *Ibid.*, p. 618.

20. The lieutenant colonel was Hilary P. Jones. Other officers definitely identified by official record include Captains Richard C. M. Page, David Watson, and William F. Dement, and Lieutenants Henry E. Blair and William A. Deas. Jones and Watson escaped that night. The former estimated the strength of the column at 1500, but was told by Dahlgren that it was 2000. (*Ibid.*, p. 211.)

21. These incidents are related in *Field and Post-Room*, edited by F. B. Kinncard and W. G. Fox (Harrisburg, Pennsylvania, 1886), I, 50.

22. Brigadier General Armistead L. Long, commanding the artillery of the Confederate Second Corps, placed the number of sharpshooters at 120. He reported: "I greatly felt the want of a few hundred infantry. With these I am sure I could have inflicted a severe chastisement upon them . . . My sharpshooters were too few, and I had too much at stake to hazard any movement against them." (See *O.R.*, Series 1, XXXIII, 210.)

The Reverend J. William Jones, D.D., writing later as secretary of the Southern Historical Society, said that he was present at Frederick's Hall at the time of Dahlgren's approach and that "there were no infantry to protect the guns." (*Southern Historical Society Papers*, XXXIV, 521, referred to hereafter as *S.H.S.P.*)

As for the number of guns involved, opinion seems to vary. Most witnesses place the total at close to 100, which would have been the case had the eight batteries of twelve guns each been complete. Mrs. Jefferson Davis, however, in *Jefferson Davis: A Memoir by His Wife* (New York, Belford Company, 1890), referred to hereafter as Davis, said there were only sixty-eight.

23. A rumor was circulated in Richmond that Lee had been captured, but this later was denied. See Richmond *Daily Dispatch*, March 1, 1864.

24. This train was due in Richmond at seven o'clock. When it failed to arrive at that hour, there was some fear that it had been captured, but later in the night news of its safety was received. See the Richmond *Daily Dispatch*, March 1, 1864.

25. *O.R.*, Series 1, XXXIII, 201.

26. Colonel Bradley T. Johnson had been placed in command of the Maryland Line and assigned to the vicinity of Hanover Court House at the direction of General Lee the preceding fall. The Line then consisted of eight companies of infantry, seven of cavalry, and a battalion of light artillery. (See *O.R.*, XXIX, Pt. II, 727.)

The function of the Maryland Line at Hanover was to guard Lee's flank toward the peninsula and the railroad bridges over the North and South Anna, in the chain of communications with Richmond.

27. Gloskoski in *O.R.*, Series 1, XXXIII, 189. Also see Spera, p. 236.

28. Gloskoski in *O.R.*, Series 1, XXXIII, 189, and Spera, p. 236, describes this Negro as a ten-year-old boy.

29. *O.R.*, Series 1, XXXIII, 1200.

30. Davis, II, 463.

31. *Records of the United States Military Telegraph.*

32. Meade, II, 168.

33. In a subsequent report of his activities, Dr. Anderson complained of the slowness with which the Confederates reacted to his warning. It was his presumption that an attack on the advancing column would be made by Rebel troops from Hanover Junction before dawn.

34. Dahlgren, p. 213.

35. *The Comanches*, by Frank M. Myers (Baltimore, Kelly, Piet and Company, 1871), p. 251.

36. This error in reporting was cited by the *Herald's* competitor, the *Times*, with the comment: "A newspaper in the habit of being beaten in the news is frequently stirred up to commit indiscretions." (See *The Rebellion Record*, VIII, 576.)

CHAPTER 7

1. Dahlgren, p. 213. This source gives the hour of the rest stop as before midnight, but all others, including Dahlgren's second in command, place it at 2:00 A.M.

2. The Richmond *Dispatch* described Kilpatrick's first stop along Brook Turnpike as on the farm of Mrs. Hillyard. From there he moved forward to the farm of Mrs. Taylor.

3. Kilpatrick's nearest approach to Richmond was somewhere in the vicinity of the present Union Theological Seminary property on Chamberlayne Avenue. See *S.H.S.P.*, XXXIV, 185.

4. These words were used by Kilpatrick in his official report. See *O.R.*, Series 1, XXXIII, 185.

5. The retreating raiders took with them considerable property from the neighborhood in which they fought. The *Dispatch* a day or two later gave a partial listing: "From Mr. Warwick they took all his teams; three mules and a horse from D. S.

Delaplane; three mules and a horse from Mrs. Hillyard; all of John Stewart's horses and mules, all his bacon, consuming or destroying fifty barrels of corn, a large quantity of wheat and oats, and other articles; the only horse from Mrs. Walton, a poor widow; all the mules and horses from J. B. Young, and carried off also his Negro butler; a pair of mules and horses from M. S. Taylor; one horse from A. D. Johnson; six mules and two horses from James A. Grant; a horse and two mules from Dr. Terrell, shot a horse in his yard, and rifled the drawers and wardrobes of his family; one mule from Mrs. Gooch, one escaping from them; two mules from Mr. Storrs; a pair of horses and a gold watch from R. C. Williamson; two Negroes from Smith and Harwood's farm, and several mules from the farms of M. Beazeley and Robert Edmond."

6. New York *Times*, as reprinted in *The Rebellion Record*, VIII, 575.

7. *Transactions of the Southern Historical Society* (Baltimore, Turnbull Brothers, 1874), I, 162. Also Davis, II, 464.

The author has been unable to determine just how much the two attacks overlapped. It would seem, however, that they went on simultaneously, that Dahlgren struck just before Kilpatrick began his withdrawal. J. R. Haws, member of the Richmond Armory Battalion, who took part in the repulse of Dahlgren, said there was some twilight left when the fighting began (see *Confederate Veteran*, Atlanta, 1890, XVII, 452), but that it was completely dark when the last attack occurred. Kilpatrick says that Dahlgren first engaged the enemy at four o'clock and, "at dark, when I withdrew my command, had driven the enemy near to the city." (*O.R.*, Series 1, XXXIII, 185.) But neither Kilpatrick nor any of his subordinate officers mentions that he heard the firing to the west of the city.

Kilpatrick was wrong, of course, in fixing the hour of the opening of Dahlgren's attack at 4:00 P.M. This was much too early. Several witnesses, including Captain John F. B. Mitchell, Dahlgren's second in command, very definitely place the beginning of the ride toward Richmond, after feeding their horses near Short Pump, at 5:00 P.M.

8. Spera, p. 242.

9. The Richmond *Dispatch*, March 3, 1864, states that Kilpatrick camped on the farm of Mrs. Eliza Crenshaw, a mile beyond Meadow Bridge, and two miles from Mechanicsville. "Their campfires were visible for some distance from the surrounding country," it reported.

10. Major J. H. Kidd, who commanded the Sixth Michigan detachment on the raid, writing in later years, said: "Kilpatrick's strategy was better than his tactics. His plan was bold in conception, but faulty in execution. It has been shown that he made a mistake in dividing his command; that he made another when he failed to order an immediate attack after his arrival before the city. His afterthought of sending Preston and Taylor, at midnight, in a snow storm, and on a night so dark it would have been impossible to keep together, to be sure of the way, or to distinguish friend from foe, to do a thing which he hesitated to do in the daytime and with his entire force, would have been a more serious blunder than either." *Personal Recollections of a Cavalryman*, p. 245.

11. *S.H.S.P.*, XXIV, 281.

12. *Personal Recollections of a Cavalryman*, p. 234.

13. From the records they left, some of Kilpatrick's men apparently thought the departure from this impromptu camp was of their own volition. One of them wrote: "About ten o'clock P.M. we are attacked in our bivouac by Confederate infantry, who are repulsed. We then move on, in the midst of a turmoil of the elements, the entire command being skillfully extricated from a perilous position, in spite of storm, mud and darkness." *History of the Eighteenth Regiment of Cavalry, Pennsylvania Volunteers, 1862-1865*, edited by Thomas J. Grier (New York, Crawford Company, 1909), p. 27.

14. It was reported in Washington that Hampton's Legion had been badly whipped by Kilpatrick, and several hundred of its number, including the leader, captured. See the New York *Times*, March 2, 1864.

15. Union and Rebel reports over the success of this expedition vary. Confederate Secretary of War Seddon, in his account

to Jefferson Davis, said Custer's men were "easily repulsed by a mere handful of half-armed artillerymen with a single gun when in a few miles of their contemplated prize of Charlottesville, and compelled to fly affrighted back to their main army." (See *O.R.*, Series 4, XXX, 325.)

16. Wade Hampton was highly pleased with the results attained by his troops. In his official report he said: "When it is taken into consideration that the cavalry with which I left camp only numbered three hundred and six men, and that this number was reduced by pickets, scouts, and broken-down horses considerably, I hope the commanding general will not regard the services performed by them as inadequate. They drove a picked division of the enemy from his camp, which they occupied from one o'clock at night till daylight. They forced this part of the enemy to take a road which he did not intend to follow, while the other force under Dahlgren was prevented from forming a junction with Kilpatrick by my troops getting between them, which brought about the precipitate retreat of Dahlgren, resulting in his death and the destruction of his command, and they bore all the hardships of a week's march with perfect cheerfulness." (*Ibid.*, Series 1, XXXIII, 202.)

17. The Southern Historical Society, making in later years a record of the damage done by Dahlgren on his raid down the James River, reported: "The disgusting orgies in which they spent three hours in the neighborhood of Dover Mills are of a character too indecent to be mentioned." (See *Transactions of the Southern Historical Society*, I, 166.

18. *The Rebellion Record*, VIII, 574.

19. *S.H.S.P.*, XXXIV, 353.

20. *Transactions of the Southern Historical Society*, I, 165.

21. In defense of Robinson, the Negro guide, the Southern Historical Society in later years recorded: "The truth was, there was a ford at that place at low water, and if the river had been fordable it was the nearest route to Belle Isle." (See *ibid.*, I, 166.)

Dr. Richard G. Crouch, who lived in the vicinity of the ford, commented in a paper read before R. E. Lee Camp

Number 1, Confederate Veterans: "It has always seemed to the writer that Richmond was saved from destruction at the hands of Dahlgren's men by the freshet of James River at the time." (*S.H.S.P.*, XXXIV, 184.)

The Reverend J. William Jones, D.D., secretary of the Southern Historical Society, visited the spot some years later and wrote about it in 1885. While there he was shown the tree on which the hanging took place, and was told by an old resident of "Unimpeachable veracity" that a ford still was in use at that point except in case of heavy rains. (*Ibid.*, XIII, 521.)

Lieutenant Reuben Bartley of the U. S. Signal Corps, riding with Dahlgren, wrote the following in the Detroit *Free Press*, March 11, 1882: "This is the most mysterious case I ever heard of. This man came down from Washington City, sent by Stanton, who was a personal friend of the colonel. He made a bargain with Kilpatrick and Dahlgren to take them to a ford at Dover Mills and take them over, when his services would cease, and in case of any mistake or treachery on his part he was to be hanged, and if it came out all right he was to receive a large sum of money. He took charge on these terms, took us safe through and had plenty of chances to make his escape, but still kept on with us. When asked why he had misled us, he did not, or could not, give a satisfactory answer. The colonel then told him he would have to carry out his part of the contract, to which the guide assented and admitted that was the agreement and made no objection to his execution. He went along to the tree without any force and submitted to his fate without a murmur."

William Preston Cabell, who in his early years lived in the neighborhood, later wrote for the Memphis *Commercial Appeal* an article in which he said residents in the vicinity allowed the Negro's body to hang there for a week "as an object lesson to impress the slaves with a new idea of Northern feeling toward the blacks." He added: "I shall never forget when a seven-year-old boy, and passing along the road one evening at twilight, how the cold chills ran over me when this gruesome spectacle met my horrified vision—the neck of the darky thrice its ordinary length and his immense pedal extremities suspended scarcely three feet from the ground." (*S.H.S.P.*, XXXIV, 356.)

Admiral Dahlgren, in *Memoir of Ulric Dahlgren*, omits all mention of the hanging of the Negro.

The Reverend Louis N. Beaudrye, writing of the hanging incident in his book on the Fifth New York Cavalry, recalled that Robinson had told them the ford was three miles below Dover Mills and added: "This was obviously false, as the river was evidently navigable to and above the place, as we saw a sloop going down the river" (p. 99). This was answered in 1885 by the Reverend J. William Jones, D.D., secretary of the Southern Historical Society, who wrote: "Every resident of this section, every schoolboy who has studied the geography of Virginia, knows that the James is not navigable above Richmond, and that no 'sloop' was ever seen at Dover Mills." (*S.H.S.P.*, XIII, 521.)

22. *O.R.*, Series 4, III, 325.

23. This is now the Westhampton section of Richmond.

24. Dr. Richard G. Crouch, Ninth Virginia Cavalry, who participated in the defense of Richmond, said Dahlgren actually got as far as the forks of the Cary Street Road. (See *S.H.S.P.*, XXXIV, 185.)

25. Lieutenant Reuben Bartley, Dahlgren's signal officer, laid the blame for the failure of the raid on Kilpatrick. Writing years later, he said: "Captain Gloskoski and myself had arranged a special code of rocket signals, so as to communicate at night and bring all the forces together in case of defeat. But Kilpatrick did not make a stand—did not return at night, and never had one rocket sent up to let us know how to get out of the scrape. He made a rather precipitate and, as one of his officers told me in Libby, demoralized run, with Hampton on his rear." (See the Detroit *Free Press*, March 11, 1882.)

26. Confederate General Fitzhugh Lee, commenting on the raid in later years, said: "The conception of the expedition, I have heard since the war, originated in General Kilpatrick's brain. It furnishes the best specimen of cavalry marching upon the Federal side; but it showed, upon the part of somebody, a

most culpable want of knowledge of data upon which to base such a movement." (Davis, II, 470.)

Seddon, the Confederate Secretary of War, said of it: "It was conducted with a timidity and feebleness that were in ludicrous contrast with the boldness of the conception and the extent of the means." See his report to Jefferson Davis of April 23, 1864, as recorded in *O.R.*, Series 4, III, 325.

27. *A Rebel War Clerk's Diary*, by J. B. Jones (New York, Old Hickory Bookshop, 1935), p. 162, referred to hereafter as Jones.

28. On the evacuation of Richmond in 1865 the local defense troops marched away with the others, most of them taking part in the final retreat and surrender at Appomattox. See John A. McAnerny's article in *Confederate Veteran*, XXIX, 20.

29. Jones, p. 164.

30. *Ibid.*

31. John A. McAnerny, in *Confederate Veteran*, XXIX, 20.

32. *S.H.S.P.*, XIII, 533.

33. This account was written by Joseph R. Haw of Hampton, Virginia, for the *Confederate Veteran*, XVI, 154, in 1908.

34. Jones, p. 389.

35. This was a reaction reported by Captain William F. Dement, who was riding with Dahlgren as a prisoner. See *Confederate Veteran*, XXIX, 21.

36. The details of Richmond's defense in the Dahlgren attack were the subject of much controversy in the pages of the *Confederate Veteran* over the years, individuals who took part arguing by pen over who had commanded a particular company or battalion and what it had done. See XV, 557; XVI, 280; XVII, 452; as well as *S.H.S.P.*, XXXIX, 63.

CHAPTER 8

1. Chesnut, p. 387.

2. Jones, p. 163.

3. Realizing Mrs. Ellery's plight after the loss of her husband,

residents of Richmond formed a committee to raise money in her behalf, collecting a total of $5402.

4. "The large concourse that attended the funeral of the fallen expressed the public lamentation," observed Jefferson Davis, in *The Rise and Fall of the Confederate Government*, by Jefferson Davis (Richmond, Virginia, Garrett & Massie, Inc.), II, 425.

5. *O.R.*, Series 1, XXXIII, 196.

6. Meade, II, 169.

7. Dr. B. H. Walker, among the local defenders who hurried forth in the emergency, kept a diary of the war years, and in it he recorded for March 2: "Yankees reported crossing Pamunkey at Dabney's Ferry and coming this way." Quotations from this diary are included in "King and Queen County," a history written by the Reverend Alfred Bagby and privately printed.

8. Pollard was greatly admired by his men. One of them said of him: "As a soldier I think he was unexcelled. He was a man who could be relied upon to do the right thing at the right time—a Virginia gentleman of gravity and of character." Dr. Richard G. Crouch in *S.H.S.P.*, XXXIV, 182.

9. *Transactions of the Southern Historical Society*, I, 168.

10. B. H. Walker, who took part in this chase, tells in his diary that he stopped at a vantage point long enough to count the Federals making up the column and found they totaled 120.

11. *The Lost Cause*, by E. A. Pollard (New York, E. B. Treat & Company, 1866), p. 501.

12. Halbach, exempt from military service on account of poor health, attended the University of Virginia prior to the war. At Stevensville he organized his pupils, ranging in age from thirteen to seventeen, into a company of home guards, but, on the arrival of Pollard's troops, had time to contact only one of them, William Littlepage. (See *The Lost Cause*, p. 504.) The teacher later became a minister of the Gospel. (*S.H.S.P.*, XIII, 550.)

13. *O.R.*, Series 1, XXXIII, 206.

14. The point at which Dahlgren had stopped is described as

"Gresham's clover field." See *Transactions of the Southern Historical Society*, I, 169.

15. E. A. Pollard, in *The Lost Cause*, p. 501, says the ambushers were divided in their opinion concerning Dahlgren's movements, some thinking he would remain in bivouac only long enough to feed his horses, others that he would wait until morning, or at least until the moon rose between 2:00 and 3:00 A.M. In this latter group was Captain Pollard, who, so thinking, went to a nearby home to rest and thus was not present when the raiders approached.

16. *Fifth New York Cavalry*, by the Reverend Louis N. Beaudrye, p. 109.

17. Exactly who fired the death-dealing blast was never known. Betty Van Lew, in her Journal, said: "By whom the fatal shot was fired it is impossible to say. I have heard no less than seven who claim that honor."

18. *O.R.*, Series 1, XXXIII, 206.

19. In his report of the affair Captain Fox was so evasive about who had been in command at the time of the ambush that there was considerable writing back and forth between him, Fitzhugh Lee, and Jeb Stuart before the laurel finally was awarded Pollard. (See *O.R.*, XXXIII, 205-07.)

CHAPTER 9

1. *Confederate Veteran*, XXVI, 353.

2. As far as the author has been able to learn from written or printed record, Butler's responsibility in the raid extended only to sending out these troops for rescue purposes. In explaining the failure of the expedition, however, Kilpatrick placed the blame on Butler for not attacking simultaneously at Bottom's Bridge and Dahlgren for not crossing the James so he could come into Richmond from the south. (See *O.R.*, XXXIII, 187.)

3. This was identified by the Richmond *Examiner*, March 5, as "Pearson's sawmill."

4. Spera, p. 248.

5. *Ibid.*, p. 244.

6. Participants on both sides placed upon Kilpatrick most of the blame for the failure of the raid. Captain John A. McAnerny, commanding the Richmond defense battalion of government clerks that blocked Dahlgren wrote in later years: "Had Kilpatrick been endowed with the courage of the dashing Dahlgren, Richmond would undoubtedly have been entered, with thirty-five thousand organized prisoners released, the city destroyed and its people thrown at the mercy of a mob of desperate and enraged Federal prisoners." (See the *Confederate Veteran*, XXIX, 20.)

7. Testimony of Lieutenant Reuben Bartley before the United States Military Commission convened to try the Lincoln assassination conspirators. See *The Assassination of President Lincoln and the Trial of the Conspirators* (Washington, D.C., U.S. Government Printing Office, 1867), p. 63.

8. *The Lost Cause*, p. 505.

9. This paper was signed: "U. Dahlgren, Colonel, Commanding." Of great significance in later developments was the transposition of the "h" and "l" in Dahlgren's name. (See *O.R.*, Series 1, XXXIII, 179.)

10. *S.H.S.P.*, XXXIV, 189.

11. *The Lost Cause*, p. 506.

12. *S.H.S.P.*, XIII, 540.

CHAPTER 10

1. *O.R.*, Series 1, XXXIII, 198.

2. *The Rebellion Record*, VIII, 572.

3. *O.R.*, Series 1, XXXIII, 216. At points along the route, as roads became more impassable and horses and mules showed signs of fatigue, wagons were lightened by throwing ammunition into streams. Twenty-six boxes were thus cast aside in one instance. (See *The Rebellion Record*, VIII, 578.)

4. *The Historical Magazine*, edited by Henry B. Dawson (Morrisania, New York, 1869), Series 2, VI, 361.

5. In a letter written for a magazine in 1870, Fitzhugh Lee gives this quotation (*S.H.S.P.*, XIII, 553) as "Jeff. Davis and Cabinet must be killed on the spot." He was wrong in including the

last three words, for these appeared only in the notation made in the memorandum book, which at the time of Lee's visit to Davis was still in the hands of Colonel R. L. T. Beale.

6. *O.R.*, Series 1, XXXIII, 217.

7. The late H. I. Hutton of Warrenton, Virginia, born in 1859, told the author during his research in connection with his earlier book, *Ranger Mosby*, that this artificial leg eventually became the property of John Ballard, one of Mosby's men who had a leg shot off in a fight in Hopewell Gap in the Bull Run Mountains.

8. *O.R.*, Series 1, XXXIII, 217.

9. *The Civil War Diary of General Josiah Gorgas*, (University, Alabama, University of Alabama Press, 1947), p. 85.

10. Private diary of Provost Marshal General, Army of the Potomac, Marsena R. Patrick, Falmouth, Stafford County, Virginia, April 10, 1863, to June 1, 1865, in the Manuscript Division, Library of Congress.

11. Statement of Edward W. Halbach in *The Lost Cause*, p. 506.

CHAPTER 11

1. The rank accorded Dahlgren by the *Examiner* was not correct. He was made a rear admiral on February 7, 1863.

2. *O.R.*, XXXIII, 218.

3. Jones, p. 166. The Lee son referred to here was General W. H. F. (Rooney) Lee, who had been captured while lying ill at the home of his wife's uncle, William F. Wickham, in Hanover County, near Richmond. When General Lee heard of the incident, he wrote his wife: "I have heard with great grief that Fitzhugh has been captured by the enemy. Had not expected that he would have been taken from his bed and carried off, but we must bear this additional affliction with fortitude and resignation and not repine at the will of God. It will eventuate in some good that we know not of now."

4. Secretary of War Stanton, in his report to the President on military operations during 1864, listed Kilpatrick's raid as one of the undertakings of greater or less magnitude "attended with disaster." (*O.R.*, Series 3, V, 504.)

5. *Confederate Veteran*, XXVI, 353.

6. *Meade's Headquarters, 1863-1865*, p. 79.

7. *O.R.*, Series 1, XXXIII, 644. Meade, with Halleck's concurrence, made the decision to bring Kilpatrick back by water. He had seen mentioned in a Richmond newspaper the possibility that the raiders would try to return by the Northern Neck, and he knew this would make it necessary for him to detach a considerable force to get them past the Confederates waiting at Fredericksburg, something that to him at the moment was not especially convenient.

8. Meade, II, 170.

9. *O.R.*, Series 1, XXXIII, 182, 649.

10. The color of the pants in which the body was clothed is another detail of the raid on which eyewitnesses failed to agree. The *Dispatch* and Betty Van Lew described them as dark blue, but the *Whig* reported they were Confederate gray. Another who saw them, John Wilder Atkinson, officer who presided over the eventual burial, said they were green, "apparently uniform pants."

11. Admiral Dahlgren, the father, described this ring as "a plain gold ring, of little worth if counted in mere dross, but inestimable as the memorial of a dearly-loved, deceased sister." He said of the missing leg and finger: "The absent limb told of battle, and proud achievement, and patriotic sacrifice; the severed finger was the work of the midnight thief." (See Dahlgren, pp. 225, 227.)

   Mrs. R. W. Barkley of Portsmouth, Virginia, born in 1866, recalls the furor over this finger-cutting act that survived in King and Queen County for many years after the war. It still sticks in her memory that the man who did it—"poor white trash," in her words—was advised to leave that area if he valued his life.

CHAPTER 12

1. Baltimore *Sun*, March 10, 1864.

2. Entry in Betty Van Lew's Journal.

3. *O.R.*, Series 2, VI, 1025.

4. *Ibid.*, p. 1024.

5. *Ibid.*, Series 1, XXXIII, 240.
6. *Ibid.*, p. 186.
7. Wistar complained that Kilpatrick made no report to him and that he did not know exactly how many men the cavalry leader had. (*Ibid.*, p. 241.) In his own report to headquarters, Kilpatrick mentioned only the total, including the force under Wistar, listing it at 2000. Actually it was nearer 4000, for Wistar gave his own strength as 2700. (*Ibid.*, pp. 186, 240.)
8. *Ibid.*, p. 242.
9. *Ibid.*, p. 245.
10. Richmond *Dispatch*, March 15, 1864.
11. *O.R.*, Series 1, XXXIII, 246.

CHAPTER 13

1. *O.R.*, Series 1, XXXIII, 175.
2. The italics appear in the report as published in *ibid.*, p. 176, but are not contained in the original now on file in the war records of the U. S. Department of Archives (XXXV, 87). Only one word was underscored in the original, and that "any" in the sentence: "All testify that he published no address whatever to his command, nor did he give any instructions."
3. *O.R.*, Series 1, XXXIII, 177.
4. The papers were photographed in the Engineer Department under the supervision of Albert H. Campbell, director of the Topographical Division. The copy sent Meade by Lee is now on file at National Archives and is so faint as to be scarcely legible.
5. *Messages and Papers of the Confederacy*, by James D. Richardson (Nashville, United States Publishing Company, 1905), II, 639.
6. *Ibid.*, I, 412.
7. *Ibid.*, II, 641.
8. *O.R.*, Series 2, VI, 1082.
9. *Ibid.*, Series 1, XXXIII, 177.
10. *Ibid.*, p. 223.

11. As far as the author has been able to ascertain, this is the last trace of the original Dahlgren papers. Their eventual fate is unknown. Only the photographic copy in the National Archives remains. If Lee returned the originals to the Adjutant General's Office as instructed, it is possible they were among the great volume of official correspondence burned in the streets of Richmond at the time of the Confederate evacuation in the spring of 1865.

   Even the photographic copies originally prepared appear to have been raided. At one time several were on file in the archives of the Southern Historical Society, but by 1906, when sought by the organization's secretary, they had disappeared. (See *S.H.S.P.*, XXXIV, 188.)

12. *O.R.*, Series 1, XXXIII, 224.

13. *Ibid.*, pp. 177, 180.

14. Meade, II, 190.

15. Private diary of M. R. Patrick in the Manuscript Division, Library of Congress.

16. *S.H.S.P.*, XXXVII, 352.

17. It was rumored that Admiral Dahlgren had promised Judge Ould he would get Lincoln to rescind the order banning the exchange of prisoners if the body were returned.

18. *O.R.*, Series 1, XXXIII, 181.

19. Betty Van Lew's Journal.

20. The author uses Miss Van Lew, an eyewitness and fellow conspirator in this undertaking, as the authority on who drove the wagon. Other contemporary recorders of the incident do not agree with her. Dr. Crouch, who served in the Ninth Virginia Cavalry and wrote of his experiences in *S.H.S.P.*, XXXIV, 179, stated the vehicle was driven by Lipscomb and a Negro, while *The Rebellion Record*, VIII, 480, attributes the action to the two Lohmans.

21. Betty Van Lew's Journal.

CHAPTER 14

1. Davis, p. 471.

2. Chesnut, p. 394.

3. *The Civil War Diary of General Josiah Gorgas*, p. 89.
4. *The Lost Cause*, p. 506.
5. *S.H.S.P.*, XIII, 554.
6. *The Historical Magazine*, Series 2, VI, 361.
7. *O.R.*, Series 1, XXXIII, 197.
8. Some of the most fantastic reasoning along this line is found in Howard Swiggett's *The Rebel Raider* (Indianapolis, The Bobbs-Merrill Company, 1934). A thorough study of the matter will reveal that Mr. Swiggett jumped to conclusions without consulting all the facts. He also is guilty of misstatement.

In the beginning he questions Jefferson Davis' interest in the secret burial of Dahlgren's body, ignoring that the Davises and the Dahlgrens were close friends at the time they were numbered among the official families of Washington.

He cites the misspelling of the name and the use of the initial "U.," factors that have gone unexplained. Who knows the circumstances under which the papers were written? Who can explain the whimsy of a twenty-one-year-old about to start on the most important assignment of his career, or the thinking of his superior officer, Kilpatrick, a man of twenty-eight? Did Dahlgren actually write them, or did some aide do so, copying the address at the direction of the colonel?

Swiggett also uses as a strong point in his argument the testimony that the address was never read to Dahlgren's men. He gives no consideration to the circumstance that the leader perhaps had no opportunity to deliver it, for the records show the first chance he had even to view his column was when it was drawn up for a fifteen-minute halt at dawn of February 29, soon after passing through Spotsylvania. Only an hour before they left Stevensburg he presented the address to Kilpatrick for his approval.

Swiggett refers to the "Special Order" found on the body and says it is vague, that it has no mention by name of the specific officers to whom the men were to look for orders. This "order," of course, was the set of instructions prepared for Mitchell, who was clearly the leader of the column proceeding with the ambulances and led horses, and it tells him in specific detail what to do.

Further reference is made to the "half-hearted" reaction of General Robert E. Lee. A more careful reading of the record will reveal that Lee's coolness was to the suggestion of executing Dahlgren's men, the slaughter of more than 100 prisoners who had been guilty only of raiding and plundering. The Confederate leader actually was much concerned over the papers. Before his death in 1870, he asked the Southern Historical Society to help him locate witnesses posted on the Dahlgren affair, explaining that "while he had never had the slightest doubt of the authenticity of the papers, he wished to furnish in his *History of the Army of Northern Virginia,* which he was purposing to write, the most indisputable proofs that the papers were genuine, and not forgeries." (See *S.H.S.P.,* XIII, 551.)

In concluding that the papers were forged, Swiggett further observes: "A memorandum book was found on Colonel Dahlgren and it is of enormous significance that the contents of it were never published." (*The Rebel Raider,* p. 215.) A complete copy of the contents of the book was made available to the public in the Richmond *Examiner,* April 1, 1864.

9. In this author's opinion, whether or not the handwriting was Dahlgren's is inconsequential. Certainly at the headquarters of a cavalry leader of Kilpatrick's rank there would have been an amanuensis who might have prepared the copies of the address and set of instructions. Whether in someone else's handwriting or however written, the guilt was there. The notes in the memorandum book were obviously the basis for the finished address and instructions, yet no one, not even his father, ever denied that these or the name of the owner of the book legibly set down on its cover were in Dahlgren's handwriting.

10. The revision of this play, described as "an historical and military drama in five acts" and written by Kilpatrick in collaboration with J. Owen Moore, was completed by the late well-known author, Christopher Morley, and was published in 1930 by Doubleday, Doran and Company, Inc., of Garden City, New York.

Index